Power and Poverty

Power and Poverty

THEORY AND PRACTICE

PETER BACHRACH

AND

MORTON S. BARATZ

New York

OXFORD UNIVERSITY PRESS

London   Toronto   1970

To our former Bryn Mawr and Haverford students who wrestled with the Problem of Power in Contemporary Society

Preface

Like so many of its kind, this book was hatched in the class-room. More than ten years in the making, it grew out of a jointly taught seminar at Bryn Mawr College for under-graduate students in political science and economics. The result of many hours of discussion, research, and refinement of written drafts, the book is truly a joint product. To put it another way, although our individual contributions are still identifiable in the final version, everything in the book bears both our imprints.

Our original interest in the subject matter is well suggested by the title of our course, The Problem of Power in Con-temporary Society. Intrigued by the controversy between "elitist" and "pluralist" students of community power, typi-fied respectively by Floyd Hunter and Robert A. Dahl, we focused initially on the limitations of each approach. Out of this came our first joint article, "Two Faces of Power," re-printed almost unchanged as Chapter I of this book.

The next step was definitional. Early on, we had been im-pressed with the many meanings assigned to power, meanings unstated as often as not. We also observed that the concepts of power, authority and influence were often used interchangeably, leading to imprecision of analysis and, not seldom, confusion. The product of our musings along these lines was "Decisions and Nondecisions: An Analytical Framework," first published in 1963 and reprinted here in modified form in Chapter II and part of Chapter III.

Neither of these articles attracted much attention at the time it first appeared. Within a few years, however, they "caught on," attracting both devotees and severe critics. The latter, by and large, acknowledged the theoretical significance of the nondecision concept, which is our major innovation, but they directed strong (and still continuing) fire at the empirical worth of the notion. How, they asked, can anyone establish the existence of a "non-event"?

The criticism, though anticipated and though inappropriately put (nondecisions are anything but non-events), was basically well taken and had to be met. As soon as possible after each of us had fulfilled independent commitments of other kinds, we rejoined forces for an empirical analysis of the relationship between the anti-poverty effort and the political process in Baltimore, Maryland. Our chief objectives were: to clarify the concept of nondecision-making, demonstrate its empirical utility, and analyze the diverse means of exercise and the impact of power and its correlates in relationship to political ideology and institutions in a community undergoing change. The city of Baltimore was admirably suited to our purposes. Throughout the period of our field research, long-submerged tensions rose to the surface, culminating in a major race riot which signaled the beginning of an overt political conflict between leaders of "inner-city" blacks and white political elites.

Our work in Baltimore, which was part of a larger evaluation of the city's "war against poverty," * was divided into two stages. Initially, we addressed ourselves to development

* The evaluation project was conducted through the Institute for Environmental Studies of the University of Pennsylvania, in association with the

of an analytical model of the political process and of a set of techniques for empirical research. The results of this work, first printed in mimeograph in a volume titled "Planning Programs for the Reduction of Poverty: Design Report" (Philadelphia, February 1967), has been substantially revised and extended in Chapters III and IV of this book. Our factual findings and interpretations appear in Chapters V-VII. (The appendices were originally distributed to a limited audience in mimeographed form.)

The materials in Chapters V through VII were gathered during 1966–68. As called for in the general contract for the evaluation project, the specific focus of the study was "the prevailing political climate" in the city of Baltimore and the ways in which it affected and was affected by the anti-poverty program.

In conformance with the approach outlined in Chapter III, the empirical phase of the political study began by focusing on several issues which either had recently been resolved in the decision-making arena or were soon to be decided. The issues included: reapportionment of municipal voting districts, decided by referendum in November 1966; pending proposals for adoption of a local "fair-housing" ordinance; a demand for greater representation of the poverty population on the Community Action Commission, the policy-making board for the Community Action Agency; the struggle for control of the fledgling Model Cities agency in Baltimore; and policy formation and implementation in the newly established Concentrated Employment Program. In addition, studies were launched into the structure and functioning of the Baltimore City Council, and of the Community Action

Urban Studies Institute of Morgan State College, under contract from the U. S. Office of Economic Opportunity (OEO-1373). The larger project was initiated and directed by Morton S. Baratz, Homer Favor, William G. Grigsby, and (during the first year only) John Kettelle. Neither the latter three nor any officials of the OEO necessarily share our conclusions nor do they bear any responsibility for errors of omission or commission.

Commission and its executive arm, the Community Action Agency.

The raw data were generated, in the main, from two kinds of source: written records, such as official documents, publications of private organizations, and local newspapers; and face-to-face interviews with upwards of 175 persons in the city—elected and appointed officials, civil servants, and spokesmen (self-styled or otherwise) of most of the identifiable interest groups in the city. In addition, questions pertaining to political attitudes and behavior were incorporated into a survey of a random, stratified sample of the city's household population.

The interviewing procedure deserves brief description, if only because the interviews were the most rewarding source of information. As is argued in Chapter III, analysis of participation in decision-making is a means not only of determining who exercises power-authority-influence and how, but also of obtaining clues as to the nature and extent of non-decision-making. With these dual objectives in mind, we consciously avoided use of a pre-determined format for interviewing. Rather, all interviews were virtually unstructured and all questions open-ended. Our gambit, to be explicit, was to encourage each respondent to describe from his own point of view how the political process works in Baltimore, that is, which issues do and which do not get into the arena for decision, and why or why not; who wants what, when, and why; and who gets what, when, and how. Once started along these lines, respondents were given virtually free rein, the interviewers limiting themselves to requests for clarification or expansion of points and inquiries as to implied but unexpressed observations.

Nearly all interviews with prominent persons, such as the Mayor, Council President, major-department heads, and key "private" persons, were conducted by at least one of the senior research workers. Decided upon in advance, this practice was adopted in order to minimize the risk that respondents would take the interviews lightly. Furthermore, in all but a few instances two or more staff members participated in the interviewing process. There were two reasons for doing this: the possibility was increased that subtleties missed by one interviewer would be noticed and pursued by another; and *ex post* impressions and judgments could be compared and contrasted. Each interviewer, in fact, made a separate set of notes on each session he attended, later producing for the file a written memorandum on what was said and his reactions to it.

As the foregoing should make clear, the empirical effort was neither hasty nor superficial. All the same, it left something to be desired. For one thing, although both of us kept in continuous touch with the political scene in Baltimore through our resident staff and through frequent visits there, we remained "outsiders," lacking the easy familiarity with people and events that is so necessary for grasping subtleties and nuances. For another thing, our coverage of "key actors" in the city, though extensive, was not exhaustive. For one reason or another, we were unable to interview some members of City Council and representatives of certain private interest groups. Finally, and perhaps most important, although we interviewed many leaders of city-wide and neighborhood political organizations, we lacked the time and money to acquire adequate knowledge of the "view from the bottom"—the political aspirations, beliefs, and attitudes of the proverbial man in the street. To a considerable extent, however, we were able to observe his political behavior.

We make no pretense to have written the final word, either on the theoretical aspects of "community power" or the political process in Baltimore. There is ample room for others who wish to revise and extend our conceptual statements, generalizations, and empirical methods. We remain firm in our belief that the path we have charted is more likely than any other to lead students of the political process to a full grasp of the phenomena of power and its correlates, how they are exercised, and with what effects upon and within the political system.

We deeply appreciate the courtesy of all the "key actors" in Baltimore who agreed to be interviewed and who so generously contributed to our understanding of the politics of their city. We also wish to thank Michel Chevalier, Brenda Davies, Ronnie Goldberg, Margaret Levi, Peter Lyman, and James Taylor, who assisted us with the interviewing and who engaged in research on various aspects of the project (see appendices). Perhaps most valuable to us were the insights they contributed during numerous intramural discussions on the theoretical underpinnings of the project and the significance of the data we were collecting.

We are also indebted to Professors Homer Favor of Morgan State College and William Grigsby of the University of Pennsylvania for valuable suggestions and criticisms throughout the course of the project. We express our appreciation to the editor of the *American Political Science Review* for permission to reprint "Two Faces of Power" (Vol. LVI, 1962), pp. 947–52; and "Decisions and Nondecisions: An Analytical Framework" (Vol. LVII), 1963), pp. 641–51. Thanks are due, too, to the editor of *Public Policy* for permission to re-work for use here, "A Power Analysis: The Shaping of Anti-poverty Policy in Baltimore" (forthcoming, Vol. XVIII, Winter 1970).

August 1969

P. B.
M. S. B.

Contents

xiii

Part One

1
Two Faces of Power

The concept of power remains elusive despite the recent and prolific outpourings of case studies on community power. Its elusiveness is dramatically demonstrated by the regularity of disagreement as to the locus of community power between the sociologists and the political scientists. Sociologically oriented researchers have consistently found that power is highly centralized, while scholars trained in political science have just as regularly concluded that in "their" communities power is widely diffused.[1] Presumably, this explains why the latter group styles itself "pluralist," its counterpart "elitist."

There seems no room for doubt that the sharply divergent

1. Compare, for example, the sociological studies of Floyd Hunter, *Community Power Structure* (Chapel Hill, 1953); Roland Pellegrini and Charles H. Coates, "Absentee-Owned Corporations and Community Power Structure," *American Journal of Sociology*, Vol. 61 (March 1956), pp. 413–19; and Robert O. Schulze, "Economic Dominants and Community Power Structure," *American Sociological Review*, Vol. 23 (February 1958), pp. 3–9; with political-science studies of Wallace S. Sayre and Herbert Kaufman, *Governing New York City* (New York, 1960); Robert A. Dahl, *Who Governs?* (New Haven, 1961); and Norton E. Long and George Belknap, "A Research Program on Leadership and Decision-Making in Metropolitan Areas" (New York, Governmental Affairs Institute, 1956). See also Nelson W. Polsby, "How To Study Community Power: The Pluralist Alternative," *Journal of Politics*, Vol. 22 (August 1960); pp. 474–84.

findings of the two groups are the product, not of sheer coin-
cidence, but of fundamental differences both in their underlying assumptions and research methodology. The political
scientists have contended that these differences in findings
can be explained by the faulty approach and presuppositions
of the sociologists. We contend in this book that the pluralists themselves have not grasped the whole truth of the matter; that while their criticisms of the elitists are sound, they,
like the elitists, utilize an approach and assumptions which
predetermine their conclusions. Our argument is cast within
the frame of our central thesis: that there are two faces of
power, neither of which the sociologists see and only one of
which the political scientists see.

I

Against the elitist approach to power several criticisms may
be, and have been leveled.[2] One has to do with its basic
premise that in every human institution there is an ordered
system of power, a "power structure" which is an integral
part and the mirror image of the organization's stratification. This postulate the pluralists emphatically—and, to our
mind, correctly—reject, on the ground that

> nothing categorical can be assumed about power in any
> community. . . . If anything, there seems to be an un-
> spoken notion among pluralist researchers that at bottom
> *nobody* dominates in a town, so that their first question
> is not likely to be, "Who runs this community?," but
> rather, "Does anyone at all run this community?" The
> first query is somewhat like, "Have you stopped beating
> your wife?," in that virtually any response short of total
> unwillingness to answer will supply the researchers with
> a "power elite" along the lines presupposed by the strati-
> fication theory.[3]

2. See especially N. W. Polsby, op. cit. p. 475f.
3. Ibid. p. 476.

Equally objectionable to the pluralists—and to us—is the sociologists' hypothesis that the power structure tends to be stable over time.

> Pluralists hold that power may be tied to issues, and issues can be fleeting or persistent, provoking coalitions among interested groups and citizens, ranging in their duration from momentary to semi-permanent. . . . To presume that the set of coalitions which exists in the community at any given time is a timelessly stable aspect of social structure is to introduce systematic inaccuracies into one's description of social reality.[4]

A third criticism of the elitist model is that it wrongly equates reputed power with actual power:

> If a man's major life work is banking, the pluralist presumes he will spend his time at the bank, and not in manipulating community decisions. This presumption holds until the banker's activities and participations indicate otherwise. . . . If we presume that the banker is "really" engaged in running the community, there is practically no way of disconfirming this notion, even if it is totally erroneous. On the other hand, it is easy to spot the banker who really *does* run community affairs when we presume he does not, because his activities will make this fact apparent.[5]

This is not an exhaustive bill of particulars; there are flaws other than these in the sociological model and methodology [6]—including some which the pluralists themselves have not noticed. To go into this would not materially serve our current purposes. Suffice it simply to observe that whatever the merits of their own approach to power, the pluralists

4. Ibid. p. 478–79.
5. Ibid. pp. 480–81.
6. See especially Robert A. Dahl, "A Critique of the Ruling-Elite Model," *American Political Science Review*, Vol. 52 (June 1958), pp. 463–69; and Lawrence J. R. Herson, "In the Footsteps of Community Power," *American Political Science Review*, Vol. 55 (December 1961), pp. 817–31.

have effectively exposed the main weaknesses of the elitist model.

As the foregoing quotations make clear, the pluralists concentrate their attention, not upon the sources of power, but its exercise. Power to them means "participation in decision-making"[7] and can be analyzed only after "careful examination of a series of concrete decisions."[8] As a result, the pluralist researcher is uninterested in the reputedly powerful. His concerns instead are to (a) select for study a number of "key" as opposed to "routine" political decisions, (b) identify the people who took an active part in the decision-making process, (c) obtain a full account of their actual behavior while the policy conflict was being resolved, and (d) determine and analyze the specific outcome of the conflict.

The advantages of this approach, relative to the elitist alternative, need no further exposition. The same may not be said about its defects, two of which seem to us to be of fundamental importance. One is that the model takes no account of the fact that power may be, and often is, exercised by confining the scope of decision-making to relatively "safe" issues. The other is that the model provides no *objective* criteria for distinguishing between "important" and "unimportant" issues arising in the political arena.

II

There is no gainsaying that an analysis grounded entirely upon what is specific and visible to the outside observer is more "scientific" than one based upon pure speculation. To put it another way,

> If we can get our social life stated in terms of activity, and of nothing else, we have not indeed succeeded in

7. This definition originated with Harold D. Lasswell and Abraham Kaplan, *Power and Society* (New Haven, 1950), p. 75.
8. Robert A. Dahl, "A Critique of the Ruling-Elite Model," loc. cit. p. 466.

measuring it, but we have at least reached a foundation upon which a coherent system of measurements can be built up. . . . We shall cease to be blocked by the intervention of unmeasurable elements, which claim to be themselves the real causes of all that is happening, and which by their spook-like arbitrariness make impossible any progress toward dependable knowledge.[9]

The question is, however, how can one be certain in any given situation that the "unmeasurable elements" are inconsequential, are not of decisive importance? Cast in slightly different terms, can a sound concept of power be predicated on the assumption that power is totally embodied and fully reflected in "concrete decisions" or in activity bearing directly upon their making?

We think not. Of course power is exercised when A participates in the making of decisions that affect B. Power is also exercised when A devotes his energies to creating or reinforcing social and political values and institutional practices that limit the scope of the political process to public consideration of only those issues which are comparatively innocuous to A. To the extent that A succeeds in doing this, B is prevented, for all practical purposes, from bringing to the fore any issues that might in their resolution be seriously detrimental to A's set of preferences.[10]

9. Arthur Bentley, *The Process of Government* (Chicago, 1908), p. 202, quoted in Polsby, op. cit. p. 481n.
10. As is perhaps self-evident, there are similarities in both faces of power. In each, A participates in decisions and thereby adversely affects B. But there is an important difference between the two: in the one case, A openly participates; in the other, he participates only in the sense that he works to sustain those values and rules of procedure that help him keep certain issues out of the public domain. True enough, participation of the second kind may at times be overt; that is the case, for instance, in cloture fights in the Congress. But the point is that it need not be. In fact, when the maneuver is most successfully executed, it neither involves nor can be identified with decisions arrived at on specific issues. For further discussion of this point, see below, pp. 43–46.

Situations of this kind are common. Consider, for example, the case—surely not unfamiliar to many in this audience —of the discontented faculty member in an academic institution headed by a tradition-bound executive. Aggrieved about a long-standing policy around which a strong vested interest has developed, the professor resolves in the privacy of his office to launch an attack upon the policy at the next faculty meeting. But, when the moment of truth is at hand, he sits frozen in silence. Why? Among the many possible reasons, one or more of these could have been of crucial importance: (a) the professor was fearful that his intended action would be interpreted as an expression of disloyalty to the institution; or (b) he decided that given the beliefs and attitudes of his colleagues on the faculty he would almost certainly constitute on this issue a minority of one; or (c) he concluded that given the nature of the law-making process in the institution his proposed remedies would be pigeonholed permanently. Whatever the case, the central point to be made is the same: to the extent that a person or group—consciously or unconsciously—creates or reinforces barriers to the public airing of policy conflicts, that person or group has power. As Professor Schattschneider has so admirably put it:

> All forms of political organization have a bias in favor of the exploitation of some kinds of conflict and the suppression of others because *organization is the mobilization of bias*. Some issues are organized into politics while others are organized out.[11]

Is such bias not relevant to the study of power? Should not the student be continuously alert to its possible existence in the human institution that he studies, and be ever prepared to examine the forces which brought it into being and sustain it? Can he safely ignore the possibility, for instance, that an individual or group in a community participates more

11. E. E. Schattschneider, *The Semi-Sovereign People* (New York, 1960), p. 71.

vigorously in supporting the *nondecision-making* process than in participating in actual decisions within the process? Stated differently, can the researcher overlook the chance that some person or association could limit decision-making to relatively noncontroversial matters, by influencing community values and political procedures and rituals, notwithstanding that there are in the community serious but latent power conflicts? [12] To do so is, in our judgment, to overlook the less apparent, but nonetheless extremely important, face of power.

III

In his critique of the "ruling-elite model," Professor Dahl argues that "the hypothesis of the existence of a ruling elite can be strictly tested only if . . . there is a fair sample of cases involving key political decisions in which the preferences of the hypothetical ruling elite run counter to those of any other likely group that might be suggested." [13] With this assertion we have two complaints. One we have already discussed, namely, in erroneously assuming that power is solely reflected in concrete decisions, Dahl thereby excludes the possibility that in the community in question there is a group capable of preventing contests from arising on issues

12. Dahl *partially* concedes this point when he observes ("A Critique of the Ruling-Elite Model," pp. 468–69) that "one could argue that even in a society like ours a ruling elite might be so influential over ideas, attitudes, and opinions that a kind of false consensus will exist—not the phony consensus of a terroristic totalitarian dictatorship but the manipulated and superficially self-imposed adherence to the norms and goals of the elite by broad sections of a community. . . . This objection points to the need to be circumspect in interpreting the evidence." But that he largely misses our point is clear from the succeeding sentence: "Yet here, too, it seems to me that the hypothesis cannot be satisfactorily confirmed without something equivalent to the test I have proposed," and that is "by an examination of a series of concrete cases where key decisions are made. . . ."
13. Op. cit. p. 466.

of importance to it. Beyond that, by ignoring the less apparent face of power Dahl and those who accept his pluralist approach are unable adequately to differentiate between a
"key" and a "routine" political decision.

Nelson Polsby proposes that "by pre-selecting as issues for
study those which are generally agreed to be significant, pluralist researchers can test stratification theory." [14] He is silent, however, on how the researcher is to determine *what* issues are "generally agreed to be significant," and on how the
researcher is to appraise the reliability of the agreement. In
fact, Polsby is guilty here of the same fault he himself has
found with elitist methodology: by presupposing that in any
community there are significant issues in the political arena,
he takes for granted the very question which is in doubt. He
accepts as issues what are reputed to be issues. As a result,
his findings are fore-ordained. For even if there is no "truly"
significant issue in the community under study, there is every
likelihood that Polsby (or any like-minded researcher) will
find one or some and, after careful study, reach the appropriate pluralistic conclusions. [15]

Dahl's definition of "key political issues" in his essay on
the ruling-elite model is open to the same criticism. He states
that it is "a necessary although possibly not a sufficient condition that the [key] issue should involve actual disagreement in preferences among two or more groups." [16] In our
view this is an inadequate characterization of a "key political issue," simply because groups can have disagreements in
preferences on unimportant as well as on important issues.
Elite preferences which border on the indifferent are certainly not significant in determining whether a monolithic
or polylithic distribution of power prevails in a given com-

14. Op. cit. p. 478.
15. As he points out, the expectations of the pluralist researcher "have seldom
been disappointed." (Ibid. p. 47.)
16. Op. cit. p. 467.

munity. Using Dahl's definition of "key political issues," the researcher would have little difficulty in finding such in practically any community; and it would not be surprising then if he ultimately concluded that power in the community was widely diffused.

The distinction between important and unimportant issues, we believe, cannot be made intelligently in the absence of an analysis of the "mobilization of bias" in the community; of the dominant values and the political myths, rituals, and institutional practices which tend to favor the vested interests of one or more groups, relative to others. Armed with this knowledge, one could conclude that any challenge to the predominant values or the established "rules of the game" would constitute an "important" issue; all else, unimportant. To be sure, judgments of this kind cannot be entirely objective. But to avoid making them in a study of power is both to neglect a highly significant aspect of power and thereby to undermine the only sound basis for discriminating between "key" and "routine" decisions. In effect, we contend, the pluralists have made each of these mistakes. That is to say, they have done just that for which Kaufman and Jones so severely taxed Floyd Hunter: they have begun "their structure at the mezzanine without showing us a lobby or foundation," [17] that is, they limited themselves to studying the issues rather than the values and biases that are built into the political system and that, for the student of power, give real meaning to those issues which do enter the political arena.

IV

There is no better fulcrum for our critique of the pluralist model than Dahl's study of power in New Haven.[18]

17. Herbert Kaufman and Victor Jones, "The Mystery of Power," *Public Administration Review*, Vol. 14 (Summer 1954), p. 207.
18. Robert A. Dahl, *Who Governs?* (New Haven, 1961).

At the outset it may be observed that Dahl does not attempt in this work to define his concept, "key political decision." In asking whether the "Notables" of New Haven are "influential overtly or covertly in the making of government decisions," he simply states that he will examine "three different 'issue-areas' in which important public decisions are made: nominations by the two political parties, urban redevelopment, and public education." These choices are justified on the ground that "nominations determine which persons will hold public office. The New Haven redevelopment program measured by its cost—present and potential—is the largest in the country. Public education, aside from its intrinsic importance, is the costliest item in the city's budget." Therefore, Dahl concludes, "It is reasonable to expect . . . that the relative influence over public officials wielded by the . . . Notables would be revealed by an examination of their participation in these three areas of activity." [19]

The difficulty with this latter statement is that it is evident from Dahl's own account that the Notables are in fact uninterested in two of the three "key" decisions he has chosen. In regard to the public school issue, for example, Dahl points out that many of the Notables live in the suburbs and that those who do live in New Haven choose in the main to send their children to private schools. "As a consequence," he writes, "their interest in the public schools is ordinarily rather slight." [20] Nominations by the two political parties as an important "issue-area" is somewhat analogous to the public schools, in that the apparent lack of interest among the Notables in this issue is partially accounted for by their suburban residence, because of which they are disqualified from holding public office in New Haven. Indeed, Dahl himself concedes that with respect to both these issues the Notables are largely indifferent: "Business leaders might ignore the

19. Ibid. p. 64.
20. Ibid. p. 70.

public schools or the political parties without any sharp awareness that their indifference would hurt their pocketbooks . . ." He goes on, however, to say that

> the prospect of profound changes [as a result of the urban-redevelopment program] in ownership, physical layout, and usage of property in the downtown area and the effects of these changes on the commercial and industrial prosperity of New Haven were all related in an obvious way to the daily concerns of businessmen.[21]

Thus, if one believes—as Professor Dahl did when he wrote his critique of the ruling-elite model—that an issue, to be considered as important, "should involve actual disagreement in preferences among two or more groups," [22] then clearly he has now for all practical purposes written off public education and party nominations as key "issue-areas." But this point aside, it appears somewhat dubious at best that "the relative influence over public officials wielded by the Social Notables" can be revealed by an examination of their *non*participation in areas in which they were not interested.

Furthermore, we would not rule out the possibility that even on those issues to which they appear indifferent, the Notables have a significant degree of *indirect* influence. We would suggest, for example, that although they send their children to private schools, the Notables do recognize that public school expenditures have a direct bearing upon their own tax liabilities. This being so, and given their strong representation on the New Haven Board of Finance,[23] the ex-

21. Ibid. p. 71.
22. Op. cit. p. 467.
23. *Who Governs?*, p. 82. Dahl points out that "the main policy thrust of the Economic Notables is to oppose tax increases; this leads them to oppose expenditures for anything more than minimal traditional city services. In this effort their two most effective weapons ordinarily are the mayor and the board of finance. The policies of the Notables are most easily achieved under

pectation must be that it is in their direct interest to play an active role in fiscal policy-making, in the establishment of the educational budget in particular. As to this, Dahl is silent: he inquires not at all into either the decisions made by the Board of Finance with respect to education nor into their impact upon the public schools.[24] Let it be understood clearly that in making these points we are not attempting to refute Dahl's contention that the Notables lack power in New Haven. What we *are* saying, however, is that this conclusion is not adequately supported by his analysis of the "issue-areas" of public education and party nomination.

The same may not be said of redevelopment. This issue is, by any reasonable standard, important for purposes of determining whether New Haven is ruled by "the hidden hand of an economic elite." [25] The Economic Notables have taken an active interest in the program and, beyond that, the socio-economic implications of it are not necessarily in harmony with the basic interests and values of businesses and businessmen.

In an effort to assure that the redevelopment program would be acceptable to what he dubbed "the biggest muscles" in New Haven, Mayor Lee created the Citizens Action Commission (CAC) and appointed to it primarily representatives of the economic elite. It was given the function of overseeing the work of the mayor and other officials involved in redevelopment, and, as well, the responsibility for organizing and encouraging citizens' participation in the program through an extensive committee system.

a strong mayor if his policies coincide with theirs or under a weak mayor if they have the support of the board of finance . . . New Haven mayors have continued to find it expedient to create confidence in their financial policies among businessmen by appointing them to the Board." (pp. 81–82)

24. Dahl does discuss in general terms (pp. 79–84) changes in the level of tax rates and assessments in past years, but not actual decisions of the Board of Finance or their effects on the public school system.

25. Ibid. p. 124.

In order to weigh the relative influence of the mayor, other key officials, and the members of the CAC, Dahl reconstructs "all the *important* decisions on redevelopment and renewal between 1950–58 . . . [to] determine which individuals most often initiated the proposals that were finally adopted or most often successfully vetoed the proposals of the others." [26] The results of this test indicate that the mayor and his development administrator were by far the most influential, and that the "muscles" on the Commission, excepting a few trivial instances, "never directly initiated, opposed, vetoed, or altered any proposal brought before them. . . ." [27]

This finding is, in our view, unreliable, not so much because Dahl was compelled to make a subjective selection of what constituted *important* decisions within what he felt to be an *important* "issue-area," as because the finding was based upon an excessively narrow test of influence. To measure relative influence solely in terms of the ability to initiate and veto proposals is to ignore the possible exercise of influence or power in limiting the scope of initiation. How, that is to say, can a judgment be made as to the relative influence of Mayor Lee and the CAC without knowing (through prior study of the political and social views of all concerned) the proposals that Lee did *not* make either because he was warned explicitly or because he anticipated that they would provoke strenuous opposition and sanctions on the part of the CAC? [28]

26. Ibid. "A rough test of a person's overt or covert influence," Dahl states in the first section of the book, "is the frequency with which he successfully initiates an important policy over the opposition of others, or vetoes policies initiated by others, or initiates a policy where no opposition appears." (Ibid. p. 66.)

27. Ibid. p. 131.

28. Dahl is, of course, aware of the "law of anticipated reactions." In the case of the mayor's relationship with the CAC, Dahl notes that Lee was "particularly skillful in estimating what the CAC could be expected to support or

In sum, because he does not recognize *both* faces of power, Dahl is in no position to evaluate the relative influence or power of the initiator and decision-maker, on the one hand, and of those persons, on the other, who may have been directly or indirectly instrumental in preventing potentially dangerous issues from being raised.[29] As a result, he unduly emphasizes the importance of initiating, deciding, and vetoing, and in the process casts the pluralist conclusions of his study into serious doubt.

V

We have argued in this chapter that a fresh approach to the study of the political process is called for, an approach which recognizes the existence of *non*decisions as well as decisions. In Chapter 3 we will try to show that nondecision-making is not only a valuable theoretical construct, but is also susceptible of empirical observation and analysis.

reject." (p. 137). However, Dahl was not interested in analyzing or appraising to what extent the CAC limited Lee's freedom of action. Because of his restricted concept of power, Dahl did not consider that the CAC might in this respect have exercised power. That the CAC did not initiate or veto actual proposals by the mayor was to Dahl evidence enough that the CAC was virtually powerless; it might as plausibly be evidence that the CAC was (in itself or in what it represented) so powerful that Lee ventured nothing it would find worth quarreling with.

29. The fact that the initiator of decisions also refrains—because he anticipates adverse reactions—from initiating other proposals does not obviously lessen the power of the agent who limited his initiative powers. Dahl missed this point: "It is," he writes, "all the more improbable, then, that a secret cabal of Notables dominates the public life of New Haven through means so clandestine that not one of the fifty prominent citizens interviewed in the course of this study—citizens who had participated extensively in various decisions—hinted at the existence of such a cabal. . ." (p. 185).

In conceiving of elite domination exclusively in the form of a conscious cabal exercising the power of decision-making and vetoing, he overlooks a more subtle form of domination; one in which those who actually dominate are not conscious of it themselves, simply because their position of dominance has never seriously been challenged.

few illustrations should clarify and enlarge our position.
 ine, first, an armed military sentry who is approached
 unarmed man in uniform. The sentry levels his gun at
 truder and calls out, "Halt or I'll shoot!" The order is
 tly obeyed. Did the sentry therefore have power and
 e it? So it would seem; but appearances could be de-
 Suppose that the intruder obeyed, not because he
 pelled to do so in the face of the threatened sanc-
 because he was himself a trained soldier for whom
 bedience to a sentry's order was part of a system of
 fully accepted.[8] If that was the case, there was no
 goals or interests between the two principals; the
 eatened sanction was irrelevant, and the result
 been the same if he, and not the intruder, had
 ed. Because the soldier put obedience to a sen-
 the top of his schedule of values, the threat of
 ations had no bearing on his behavior. In such
 it cannot be said that the guard exerted

 uppose that a second man approaches the sen-
 e first, is ordered to stop or be shot. The sec-
 ores the order, attempts to smash through
 orthwith fatally wounded. If we assume that
 ention was to sabotage the military installa-
 no doubt that his and the sentry's values
 lict. Even so, the sentry's fatal shot did *not*
 ise of power. For it did not bring about
 der—and it did not because, apparently,
 entry to the base more highly than ei-
 sentry's order or his own well-being.
 at a third man approaches the sentry
 to die but cannot bring himself to the
 He therefore deliberately ignores the
 s duly shot to death. Did someone in

 n represents another kind of interpersonal re-
 discussed below.

2
Key Concepts:
Power, Authority, Influence, Force

In recent years a rich outpouring of case studies on community decision-making has been combined with a noticeable
lack of generalizations based on them. One reason for this is
a commonplace: we have no general theory, no broad-gauge
model in terms of which widely different case studies can be
systematically compared and contrasted.

Among the obstacles to the development of such a theory
is a good deal of confusion about the nature of power and of
the things that differentiate it from the equally important
concepts of force, influence, and authority. These terms have
different meanings and are of varying relevance; yet in
nearly all studies of community decision-making published
to date, power and influence are used almost interchangeably and force and authority are neglected.[1] The researchers
thereby handicap themselves. For they utilize concepts which
are at once too broadly and too narrowly drawn: too
broadly, because important distinctions between power and

1. See, for example, Floyd Hunter, *Community Power Structure* (Chapel Hill,
1953); and Robert A. Dahl, *Who Governs?* (New Haven, 1961).

influence are brushed over; and too narrowly, because other concepts are disregarded—concepts which, had they been brought to bear, might have altered the findings radically.

Many investigators have also mistakenly assumed that power and its correlatives are activated and can be observed only in decision-making situations. As we argued in Chapter 1, they have overlooked the equally, if not more important area of what we have called nondecision-making, that is, the practice of limiting the scope of actual decision-making to "safe" issues by manipulating the dominant community values, myths, and political institutions and procedures. To pass over this is to neglect one whole "face" of power.[2]

Finally, the case studies are often based upon inarticulate, perhaps unsound, premises which predetermine the findings of fact.[3] A variety of complex factors affect decision-making: the social, cultural, economic, and political backgrounds of the individual participants; the values of the decision-making body as an entity in itself; the pressures brought to bear on the decision-makers, individually and collectively, by groups at interest; and so on. To say, as some do, that these factors are equally important is as far from the mark as to assume, as others do, that only one is of overriding significance.[4]

What is required, then, is a model in terms of which the determinants both of decision- and nondecision-making can be appraised, taking full account of the distinct concepts of power, force, influence, and authority. In this chapter we are not so ambitious. We attempt only to lay some of the groundwork for a model, seeking (1) to clarify the attributes of what we consider key concepts for any study of decision- and

2. A somewhat similar view, arrived at independently, may be found in Thomas J. Anton, "Power, Pluralism, and Local Politics," *Administrative Science Quarterly*, Vol. 7 (March 1963), p. 453.

3. See above, pp. 4–6.

4. *Cf.* Peter Rossi, "Community Decision-Making," in Roland Young (ed.), *Approaches to the Study of Politics* (Evanston, Ill., 1958), p. 359.

nondecision-making and the essential di
and (2) to show how these concepts ca
tematically and effectively in case st

I

It is customary to say that this
power," the implication being
possession which enables its
future Good.[5] Another way
view is to say that power
can belong to a person or

For at least three reas
it fails to distinguish c
power over matter; ar
or social] sense cann
intended effects in
other persons. . . .
is measured by th
erroneous; one
relation to so
common con
that possess
power is ta
tion is fa
tribute
contra
the re
the

2
Key Concepts:
Power, Authority, Influence, Force

In recent years a rich outpouring of case studies on community decision-making has been combined with a noticeable lack of generalizations based on them. One reason for this is a commonplace: we have no general theory, no broad-gauge model in terms of which widely different case studies can be systematically compared and contrasted.

Among the obstacles to the development of such a theory is a good deal of confusion about the nature of power and of the things that differentiate it from the equally important concepts of force, influence, and authority. These terms have different meanings and are of varying relevance; yet in nearly all studies of community decision-making published to date, power and influence are used almost interchangeably and force and authority are neglected.[1] The researchers thereby handicap themselves. For they utilize concepts which are at once too broadly and too narrowly drawn: too broadly, because important distinctions between power and

1. See, for example, Floyd Hunter, *Community Power Structure* (Chapel Hill, 1953); and Robert A. Dahl, *Who Governs?* (New Haven, 1961).

influence are brushed over; and too narrowly, because other concepts are disregarded—concepts which, had they been brought to bear, might have altered the findings radically.

Many investigators have also mistakenly assumed that power and its correlatives are activated and can be observed only in decision-making situations. As we argued in Chapter 1, they have overlooked the equally, if not more important area of what we have called nondecision-making, that is, the practice of limiting the scope of actual decision-making to "safe" issues by manipulating the dominant community values, myths, and political institutions and procedures. To pass over this is to neglect one whole "face" of power.[2]

Finally, the case studies are often based upon inarticulate, perhaps unsound, premises which predetermine the findings of fact.[3] A variety of complex factors affect decision-making: the social, cultural, economic, and political backgrounds of the individual participants; the values of the decision-making body as an entity in itself; the pressures brought to bear on the decision-makers, individually and collectively, by groups at interest; and so on. To say, as some do, that these factors are equally important is as far from the mark as to assume, as others do, that only one is of overriding significance.[4]

What is required, then, is a model in terms of which the determinants both of decision- and nondecision-making can be appraised, taking full account of the distinct concepts of power, force, influence, and authority. In this chapter we are not so ambitious. We attempt only to lay some of the groundwork for a model, seeking (1) to clarify the attributes of what we consider key concepts for any study of decision- and

2. A somewhat similar view, arrived at independently, may be found in Thomas J. Anton, "Power, Pluralism, and Local Politics," *Administrative Science Quarterly*, Vol. 7 (March 1963), p. 453.
3. See above, pp. 4–6.
4. *Cf.* Peter Rossi, "Community Decision-Making," in Roland Young (ed.), *Approaches to the Study of Politics* (Evanston, Ill., 1958), p. 359.

nondecision-making and the essential differences among them, and (2) to show how these concepts can be utilized more systematically and effectively in case studies.

I

It is customary to say that this or that person or group "has power," the implication being that power, like wealth, is a possession which enables its owner to secure some apparent future Good.[5] Another way of expressing the same point of view is to say that power is a "simple property . . . which can belong to a person or group considered in itself." [6]

For at least three reasons this usage is unacceptable. First, it fails to distinguish clearly between power over people and power over matter; and "power in the political [or economic or social] sense cannot be conceived as the ability to produce intended effects in general, but only such effects as involve other persons. . . ." [7] Second, the view that a person's power is measured by the total number of desires that he achieves is erroneous; one cannot have power in a vacuum, but only in relation to someone else. Third and most important, the common conception of the phenomenon mistakenly implies that possession of (what appear to be) the instruments of power is tantamount to possession of power itself. Such a notion is false because it ignores the fundamental relational attribute of power: that it cannot be possessed; that, to the contrary, the successful exercise of power is dependent upon the relative importance of conflicting values *in the mind of the recipient* in the power relationship.

5. Thomas Hobbes, as paraphrased by C. J. Friedrich, *Constitutional Government and Politics* (New York, 1937), p. 12.
6. Harold D. Lasswell and Abraham Kaplan, *Power and Society* (New Haven, 1950), p. 75, draw this implication from the definition of power, that is, "the production of intended effects," in Bertrand Russell, *Power: A New Social Analysis* (New York, 1938), p. 35.
7. Lasswell and Kaplan, loc. cit.

A few illustrations should clarify and enlarge our position. Imagine, first, an armed military sentry who is approached by an unarmed man in uniform. The sentry levels his gun at the intruder and calls out, "Halt or I'll shoot!" The order is promptly obeyed. Did the sentry therefore have power and exercise it? So it would seem; but appearances could be deceiving. Suppose that the intruder obeyed, not because he felt compelled to do so in the face of the threatened sanction, but because he was himself a trained soldier for whom prompt obedience to a sentry's order was part of a system of values he fully accepted.[8] If that was the case, there was no conflict of goals or interests between the two principals; the sentry's threatened sanction was irrelevant, and the result would have been the same if he, and not the intruder, had been unarmed. Because the soldier put obedience to a sentry's order at the top of his schedule of values, the threat of severe deprivations had no bearing on his behavior. In such circumstances it cannot be said that the guard exerted power.

Let us now suppose that a second man approaches the sentry and, like the first, is ordered to stop or be shot. The second stranger ignores the order, attempts to smash through the gate, and is forthwith fatally wounded. If we assume that the intruder's intention was to sabotage the military installation, we can have no doubt that his and the sentry's values were in direct conflict. Even so, the sentry's fatal shot did *not* constitute an exercise of power. For it did not bring about compliance to his order—and it did not because, apparently, the intruder valued entry to the base more highly than either obedience to the sentry's order or his own well-being.

Suppose, finally, that a third man approaches the sentry box, a man who wants to die but cannot bring himself to the act of self-destruction. He therefore deliberately ignores the sentry's command and is duly shot to death. Did someone in

8. Agreement based upon reason represents another kind of interpersonal relationship—authority—which is discussed below.

this situation have power and exercise it? As we see it, the "victim" did—for it was he, cognizant of the conflict of values between himself and the guard, who utilized the latter's supposed sanction to achieve his own objective.[9]

We reiterate that power is relational, as opposed to possessive or substantive. Its relational characteristics are threefold. First, in order for a power relationship to exist there must be a conflict of interests or values between two or more persons or groups. Such a divergence is a necessary condition of power because, as we have suggested, if A and B are in agreement as to ends, B will freely assent to A's preferred course of action; in which case the situation will involve authority rather than power.[10] Second, a power relationship exists only if B actually bows to A's wishes. A conflict of interests is an insufficient condition, since A may not be able to prevail upon B to change his behavior. And if B does not comply, A's policy will either become a dead letter or will be effectuated through the exercise of force rather than through power.[11] Third, a power relationship can exist only if one of the parties can threaten to invoke sanctions: power is "the process of affecting policies of others with the help of (. . . threatened) severe deprivations for nonconformity with the policies intended."[12] It must be stressed, however, that while the availability of sanctions—that is, of any promised reward or penalty by which an actor can maintain effective

9. It might be argued that the "victim" did not actually exercise power in this instance, because he had no sanctions with which to threaten the sentry. This objection misses the obvious point: the "victim" threatened the guard with severe deprivations (dishonor, imprisonment) if the guard did not perform his soldierly duty by complying with the "victim's" command that he (the "victim") be killed.

10. See Section IV below.

11. See Section II below.

12. Lasswell and Kaplan, *op. cit.*, p. 76. We have deleted "actual or" from the parenthetical expression because *actual* deprivation for nonconformity is a property of force, rather than power. This point is discussed further below.

The Lasswell-Kaplan definition is open to another criticism. They observe (p. 77) that "to have power is to be taken into account in others' acts (pol-

control over policy—is a necessary condition of power, it is not sufficient. It is necessary simply because the threat of sanctions is what differentiates power from influence [13]; it is insufficient because the availability of a sanction endows A with power over B only if the following conditions are met:

(a) The person threatened is aware of what is expected of him. In a power situation there must be clear communication between the person who initiates policy and the person who must comply.[14] If our imaginary sentry challenges a man who understands no English or is perhaps deaf, the sentry has—at least at the moment he issues his order—no power. In other words, power has a rational attribute: for it to exist, the person threatened must comprehend the alternatives which face him in choosing between compliance and noncompliance.

(b) The threatened sanction is *actually* regarded as a deprivation by the person who is so threatened. A threat by the President to "purge" a Congressman for failure to support the Administration's legislative program would be to no avail if the Congressman reckoned that his chances for re-el-

icies)." Strictly construed, this must mean that any and every person or group involved—in whatever degree—in decision-making must have power. Is not the farmer who markets .001 per cent of the total supply of wheat "taken into account" by other buyers and sellers in just the same sense—though not, of course, in the same degree—as is the General Motors Corporation in the determination of automobile prices? Or, to change the illustration, is it not the case that, in the literal interpretation of the word, nonvoters as well as voters "participate," and therefore have power, in deciding close elections? We should think so. But if this is what is meant by power, how can we avoid concluding that no matter where we look, we shall always find that power is broadly diffused? To rephrase, if (a) we analyze the distribution of power solely in terms of decision-making and (b) we ascribe power to all who participate in whatever measure or with whatever "weight" ("The weight of power is the degree of participation in the making of decisions . . ." [ibid.], then (c) do we not necessarily prejudge that power in real-world situations will be widely dispersed?

13. See Part III below.

14. See Richard E. Neustadt, *Presidential Power* (New York, 1960), p. 21. Compare Thomas C. Schelling, *The Strategy of Conflict* (Cambridge, Mass., 1960), pp. 38–39.

ection would be increased rather than reduced by Presidential intervention.

(c) The person threatened has greater esteem for the value which would be sacrificed should he disobey than for another value which would be forgone should he comply. Fear of physical injury did not deter those Southern Negro "sitters-in" who put greater store by the righteousness of their cause. It is worth noting at this stage that threatened deprivations are often ineffectual because the policy-initiator, in deciding what sanction to invoke, mistakenly projects his own values into the minds of his subjects.[15]

(d) The person threatened is persuaded that the threat against him is not idle, that his antagonist would not hesitate *in fine* actually to impose sanctions. To illustrate, if a famous general calculates that the President lacks the will or the popular support to employ his Constitutional prerogatives, he may ignore—even defy—the President's policy instructions.[16] Or, again, the success of a resistance movement based on the principle of nonviolence rests in large measure upon the assumption that those who can invoke sanctions will refrain from doing so, that value conflicts

15. This error, compounded by that of regarding power as something which is possessed, may well have underlain the policy of the United States toward Chiang Kai-shek during the period (1944–49) of the Chinese civil war. It is entirely possible, that is to say, that in providing substantial amounts of armament to the Kuomintang regime, we mistook the instruments of power for power itself; and, in addition, by interpreting the Kuomintang-Communist struggle in terms of our own values, we utterly misread the temper of the great majority of the Chinese people.

The abortive invasion of Cuba in April 1961 is perhaps another example of the inherent danger in projecting our values onto a populace holding a different collection of interests. Looking at the great body of Cuban nationals who were apparently bereft both of individual freedom and personal dignity, we concluded that we need only provide the opportunity, the spark, which would ignite nation-wide uprisings against the Castro regime. Hindsight has indicated how badly we misread popular feeling in Cuba. See Stewart Alsop, "Lessons of the Cuban Disaster," *Saturday Evening Post,* 24 June 1961, pp. 26–27.

16. Neustadt, op. cit. pp. 12–13. On the general point, see also Schelling, op. cit. p. 6.

within A will prevent him from carrying out his threat against B. In point are the Indians who sat on the railroad tracks in defiance of the British and got away with it because (as the Indians well knew) the British put a higher value on human life than on obedience to their orders.[17]

We can now draw together the several elements of our conception of power. A power relationship exists when (a) there is a conflict over values or course of action between A and B; (b) B complies with A's wishes; and (c) B does so because he is fearful that A will deprive him of a value or values which he regards more highly than those which would have been achieved by noncompliance.[18]

Several points must be made in reference to this defini-

17. The point is also well illustrated by Franco-American policy differences in the early 1960s. Committed both to the defense of Western Europe and to strict limitation on the number of nations with independent nuclear forces, the United States was caught in a dilemma in its dealings with General de Gaulle. In the words of a contemporary observer, "De Gaulle . . . has played a judo trick on the United States . . . [He] means to fashion his 'European construction,' based on the *force de frappe* and the Franco-German axis and excluding the British and Americans. And he means to do this *under the umbrella of the American nuclear deterrent* . . . there is precious little the Kennedy Administration can do about de Gaulle's judo trick—short of removing its nuclear protection. And this has not even been seriously considered. . . . 'We're a bit like that little Dutch boy with his finger in the dike,' says one Kennedy adviser. Remove the American commitment to defend Euorpe, and the result is unmitigated disaster, not only to Europe but to the United States. Thus the United States, like the little Dutch boy, is immobilized. The strongest power in the Western alliance has amazingly little bargaining power in the alliance." Stuart Alsop, "Should We Pull Out of Europe?" *Saturday Evening Post*, 13 April 1963, p. 80. Emphasis in original.

The main point is made more pithily by "President Hudson" in Allen Drury's novel, *A Shade of Difference* (New York, 1962), p. 82: "The more real power you have, the less you can afford to exercise it, and the less real power you have, the more you can throw it around."

For further discussion of the relationship between power and commitment, see E. Abramson *et al.*, "Social Power and Commitment Theory," *American Sociological Review*, Vol. 23 (February 1958), pp. 15–22.

18. With Lasswell and Kaplan, op. cit. p. 16, we define a value as "a desired event—a goal event. That X values Y means that X acts so as to bring about the consummation of Y."

tion. First, in speaking of power relations, one must take care not to overstate the case by saying that A has power over B merely because B, anxious to avoid sanctions, complies with a given policy proclaimed by A. This could well be an inaccurate description of their relationship, since A's power with respect to B may be extremely limited in scope, that is, in range of values affected.[19] Thus, the power of a traffic policeman over a citizen may be confined to the latter's activities as a motorist—and no more than that. Moreover, in appraising power relationships account must be taken of the weight of power, i.e. the degree to which values are affected, and of its domain, i.e. the number of persons affected.[20] For example, the power of the chairman of the House Committee on Ways and Means is limited mainly to fiscal affairs; but within this scope he wields immense power in the determination of Federal tax and expenditure policies (weight), which affect a vast number of persons—up to and including at times the President himself (domain).

Furthermore, account must be taken of what Friedrich has dubbed the "rule of anticipated reactions." [21] The problem posed by this phenomenon is that an investigation might reveal that, though B regularly accedes to A's preferred courses of action, A in fact lacks power over B because A just as regularly tailors his demands upon B to dimensions he thinks B will accept. As an illustration, if the President submits to the Congress only those bills likely to be palatable to a majority of lawmakers, he can hardly be said to have power over the Congress simply because all his proposals are enacted into law.

19. Ibid. p. 76.
20. Ibid. p. 77.
21. Op. cit. pp. 17–18. A corollary proposition could be called the "rule of *mis*anticipated reactions." We refer to a situation in which one person grudgingly conforms to what he *thinks* another wants, but finds after the fact either that he misread the other's preferences or that the latter never intended to invoke sanctions for behavior contrary to his preferences.

There is an additional dimension to anticipated reactions. It is often inferred that because a group is unorganized, inarticulate, and lacks effective access to key centers of decision-making, it is totally powerless in every sense of the word. The inference could be incorrect. An investigation might well reveal that decision-makers alter their policy choices out of deference to the supposedly powerless group, in anticipation that failure to do so would bring on severe deprivations, e.g. riots, boycotts, and so on. Here is a situation in which policy-makers' recognition of the possibility of future sanctions (*potential* power) results in "exercise" of power in the present. Potential power, that is, becomes actual power, even in circumstances where those who "threaten" the sanctions have not actually invoked them.

We must also take note of *latent* power. It is commonly supposed that anyone who possesses what appear to be important instruments for exercising power, such as wealth, high social rank, or a well-stocked military arsenal, necessarily puts them to work. C. Wright Mills, for example, has argued that the "power elite" in America is made up of those persons who command the major institutions—great corporations, the military establishment, and the political bureaucracy. In his words, "Not all power . . . is anchored in and exercised by means of such institutions, but only within and through them can power be more or less continuous and important." [22] Although his point has merit, Mills and others tend to overlook that those who have the means for threatening sanctions may and often do abstain from doing so. Their power is *latent,* rather than real. We must mention, however, that the existence of latent power can result in its actual, if unintended, exercise. For instance, the managing director of a community's largest business firm may choose to abstain from exercising power in the resolution of local political issues. Yet the resources at his disposal

22. C. Wright Mills, *The Power Elite* (New York, 1954), p. 9.

are so great—that is, he has so much latent power—that others in the locality may regularly defer to his (real or imagined) preferences. In cases like this, B is the recipient in a power relationship with A, even though A did not "exercise" power in Lasswell and Kaplan's sense of participation in decision-making with respect to policies that affect B.

II

In Robert Bierstedt's opinion, "force is manifest power . . . Force . . . means the reduction or limitation or closure or even total elimination of alternatives to the social action of one person or group by another person or group. 'Your money or your life' symbolizes a situation of naked force, the reduction of alternatives to two." [23] Force, in short, is power exercised.

We reject this view. As we see it, the essential difference between power and force is simply that in a power relationship one party obtains another's compliance, while in a situation involving force one's objectives must be achieved, if at all, in the face of the other's *non*compliance.[24] Thus, if A's demand for B's money or his life prompts B to surrender his wallet, A has exercised power—he has won B's compliance by threat of even more severe deprivations. But if A must kill B to get the money, A has to resort to force—he must actually invoke the threatened sanction—and thereby perhaps expose himself to more severe deprivations too. By the same token, if and when thermonuclear weapons are transformed from instruments of a policy of deterrence into activated missiles of death, power will have given way to force.

There is another difference between the two concepts. A

23. "An Analysis of Social Power," *American Sociological Review*, Vol. 15 (December 1950), p. 733.
24. A major defect of Lord Russell's conception of power (see above, note 6) is that it utterly ignores this distinction. One can produce an "intended effect" through the exercise of either power or force.

person's scope of decision-making is radically curtailed under
the duress of force; once the fist, the bullet, or the missile is
in flight, the intended victim is stripped of choice between
compliance and noncompliance. Where power is being exercised, the individual retains this choice. Put another way, in
a power relationship it is B who chooses what to do, while in
a force relationship it is A.[25]

It follows from the foregoing that *manipulation* is an aspect of force, not of power. For, once the subject is in the
grip of the manipulator, he has no choice as to course of action. It can be said, therefore, that force and manipulation
(as a sub-concept under it) are, in contrast to power, nonrational.

An additional distinguishing attribute of force is that in
some circumstances it is nonrelational. For instance, if B is
shot in the back by an unknown robber, he and his assailant
have only a minimal interrelationship—especially when compared with a power confrontation where B must decide
whether to accede to A's demands. A similarly minimal relationship obtains in cases involving manipulation, where
compliance is forthcoming in the absence of recognition on
the complier's part either of the source or the exact nature of
the demand upon him.

In short, force and manipulation, like power, involve a
conflict of values; but unlike power, they are nonrational
and tend to be nonrelational.

A number of implications may be drawn from this reasoning. One is that the actual application of sanctions is an admission of defeat by the would-be wielder of power. And so
it is, to the extent that the prior *threat* of sanctions failed to
bring about the desired behavior. A good case in point is the

25. It is often true, when force is operative, that A gives B the option to comply with his demands *between* blows. In such circumstances, should B bend
to A's wishes, he does so out of fear of further sanctions, in which case force
is transformed into power.

action of President Harry S Truman in 1951 when he relieved General Douglas MacArthur of his command in the
Pacific on grounds of insubordination. By continuing to air
in public his policy differences with the Administration,
MacArthur virtually compelled Truman to dismiss him. The
President's decision to apply sanctions was, however, an admission of defeat, an implicit recognition that he could not,
by power or authority, obtain MacArthur's compliance to
the Administration's policy of a negotiated settlement of the
Korean hostilities. To be sure, policy defeats of this kind
may prove to be only partial. If the resort to force against
one party effectively deters noncompliance on the part of
others, now or in future, the employment of sanctions becomes a fresh declaration of the existence of power. This is,
of course, the rationale of nearly all who undertake punitive
actions against others: the *use* of force in one situation increases the credibility of *threats* to use it in others.

At the same time, it is important to recognize that resort
to force can result in a loss of power. Two cases can be distinguished. First, the invocation of sanctions often causes a
radical reordering of values within the coerced person (as
well as in those persons who identify closely with him),
thereby undermining the pre-existing power relationship. A
good illustration is provided by the largely abortive attempt
of the Nazis during World War II to pacify the populations
of occupied countries by killing civilian hostages. Contrary
to German expectations, this policy produced a marked stiff-
ening of resistance; evidently, the number of "prisoners"
who put a higher value on freedom than on life itself rose
sharply. Second, the deprivation may prove in retrospect far
less severe than it appeared in prospect, as a result of which
future noncompliance is not discouraged and may even be
encouraged. For example, a child whose punishment for mis-
behavior is the temporary loss of a prized toy may find, *ex
post facto,* that the loss is entirely bearable, that the satisfac-

tions he gained from acting up are greater at the margin than the alternative forgone. In such circumstances, obviously, future defiance of parental orders is more likely than not.

Just as power may be lessened when force is resorted to, so also may power be lessened when it is successfully exercised, that is, when compliance is obtained by mere threat of sanctions. As an illustration, Presidents of the United States have traditionally sought to exercise power over recalcitrant Congressmen by withholding patronage. But as a President exchanges a job appointment for votes—that is, as he successfully utilizes this source of power—his reserves for effecting further compliance dry up. As a corollary, repeated threats to invoke sanctions—threats never carried out—will gradually lose credibility in the minds of those threatened, until at length the threats cannot produce the desired behavior. This, in the view of many, was the basic flaw in the implementation of the stated American policy during the late 1950s of "massive retaliation at times and in places of our own choosing." [26] The same phenomenon applies to interpersonal relationships: a threat to withdraw one's love for another may be highly potent the first time, yet prove totally ineffectual if used again.

III

One person has *influence* over another within a given scope to the extent that the first, without resorting to either a tacit or an overt threat of severe deprivations, causes the second to change his course of action. Thus, power and influence are alike in that each has both rational and relational attributes. But they are different in that the exercise of power depends upon potential sanctions, while the exercise of influence does

26. One of the more penetrating critiques along these lines may be found in General Maxwell D. Taylor, *The Uncertain Trumpet* (New York, 1959).

not. And there is an important difference between influence and manipulation: in situations involving the latter, but not the former, A seeks to disguise the nature and source of his demands upon B and, if A is successful, B is totally unaware that something is being demanded of him.

Although power and influence can and must be distinguished, the line between them is usually difficult to draw. This is especially true where B's reasons for acting in accordance with A's wishes are confused or multiple; in such circumstances B himself will be unable honestly to say whether his behavior was prompted by a fear of sanctions or, rather, by his esteem for "higher" values (e.g. wealth, respect, power, wisdom) than the one immediately at stake. Does the ambitious young man who submits unhappily to the every dictate of his rich uncle do so because he admires wealthy men (influence) or because he feels that unquestioning obedience is the price of a generous inheritance in the future (power)? Does the Majority Leader who unwillingly manages an Administration bill in the Senate do so because he is in awe of the Presidency and hence of the man who occupies the office (influence), or because he fears the President will actually punish him for noncompliance (power)? To say that the decisive test in situations like these turns on whether compliance is "voluntary" or "involuntary" is, in our judgment, not particularly helpful.[27]

The difficulty in distinguishing sharply and clearly between power and influence is further complicated by the fact

27. According to Bierstedt, op. cit. p. 731, ". . . influence is persuasive while power is coercive. We submit voluntarily to influence while power requires submission." In our view, if B submits voluntarily, power is operative; but if he submits under duress, force is operative.

It is worth noting that under our definition it would be incorrect to say that Marx "influenced" Lenin, or that Haydn "influenced" Mozart, or that Jesus Christ "influenced" the Conquistadores. In each of these cases the second *shared* the values of the first, that is, the relationship involved neither power nor influence, but *authority*. See Section IV below.

that the two are often mutually reinforcing, that is, power
frequently generates influence and vice versa. On this score,
the case of Senator Joseph R. McCarthy of Wisconsin is especially instructive.[28] Shrewdly posing as the principal defender of the national security at the very moment when
that became the dominant social value *vice* the inviolability
of civil liberties, McCarthy managed for a period to stifle virtually all opposition to himself and what he stood for (influence). From this base he was able to gain power, that is, to
affect the making of actual decisions (votes in the Senate,
acts of the Executive, etc.) by threats of severe deprivations
(intervention in state political campaigns, destruction by accusation of the careers of appointive officials, etc.). By the
same token, however, as public fears about national security
subsided and concern for civil liberties grew, McCarthy's capacity to influence others sharply waned—and so, too, did his
power.

Just because the distinction between power and influence
is often blurred does not, however, lessen the importance of
making the distinction. Nikita Khrushchev had little or no
influence over Americans, yet it is obvious that in his time
he exercised considerable power over us. On the other hand,
the Supreme Court of the United States has widespread influence (and authority) over us both individually and collectively; its power is slight indeed.

IV

While authority is closely related to power, it is not a form
thereof; it is, in fact, antithetical to it.[29] In saying this, we
reject both the traditional definition of authority as "formal

28. See Richard H. Rovere, *Senator Joe McCarthy* (New York, 1959).
29. C. J. Friedrich, "Authority, Reason and Discretion," in C. J. Friedrich,
Authority, 9th ed. (Cambridge, Mass., 1958), p. 37.

power"[30] and that which conceives it as "institutionalized power."[31]

To regard authority as a form of power is, in the first place, not operationally useful. If authority is "formal power," then one is at a loss to know who has authority at times when the agent who possesses "formal power" is actually powerless. To say that Captain Queeg continued to have authority on the USS *Caine* after he was relieved of his command by the mutineers is to create needless confusion. Furthermore, to define authority as "formal power" is to fail to delineate the bounds of authority, other perhaps than to say that it ends where "real power" begins. For those who believe in limited or constitutional government such a construction is unthinkable.

To argue that "formal power" is circumscribed by law is also no answer. For it assumes without warrant the legitimacy of law. A policeman who demands obedience in the name of a law that is considered basically unjust will possess little authority in the eyes of persons steeped in the Anglo-American legal tradition. Nor is the problem completely solved by conceiving of authority in terms of constitutional legitimacy. Such a conception presupposes that all members of the community give allegiance to the Constitution and the courts which interpret it. Do Federal courts have the authority to issue desegregation orders to Southern school districts? According to many Southerners, including some learned in the law, the answer is in the negative.

Friedrich's analysis of authority seems to us the most appropriate. He defines the concept as "a quality of communication" that possesses "the potentiality of reasoned elaboration."[32] Like power, authority is here regarded as a

30. Lasswell and Kaplan, op. cit. p. 133.
31. Bierstedt, op. cit. p. 733.
32. *Authority*, pp. 36, 35.

relational concept: it is not that A possesses authority, but that B regards A's communication as authoritative. Also like power, an authority relationship implies rationality—although of a different order. That is, in a situation involving power, B is rational in the sense that he chooses compliance instead of defiance because it seems the less of two evils.[33] In a situation involving authority, B complies because he recognizes that the command is reasonable in terms of his own values; in other words, B defers to A, not because he fears severe deprivations but because his decision can be rationalized.[34] It is not essential, however, that A's directive be supported by reasoning; it is sufficient that the potentiality of such reasoning be present and recognized.[35]

If B believes that A's communication allows for reasoned elaboration when in fact it does not, it is "false" authority.[36] When the source of obedience shifts from "genuine" to "false" authority and B realizes that the communication cannot be elaborated effectively, then a relationship initially involving authority has been transformed into one involving power. For example, if a policeman demanded entrance to your house, you would probably comply on the implicit assumption that his demand was potentially supportable by reason. However, should you discover, once he was in, that

33. As is perhaps obvious, if B chooses to defy A, the relationship no longer will involve power. This notion of rationality of choice is analogous to Thomas Hobbes's treatment of the relationship between fear and liberty. "Feare, and Liberty," he wrote, "are consistent; as when a man throweth his goods into the Sea for *feare* the ship should sink, he doth it neverthelesse very willingly, and may refuse to doe it if he will: It is therefore the action, of one that was free." *Leviathan*, Everyman Edition, p. 110.

34. Friedrich, *Authority*, p. 36. Reasoning also underlies the difference between authority and influence. Thus, if B complies with A's demand neither because he fears deprivations nor because his compliance is based upon reasoning, B has been influenced. This distinction will be further elaborated below.

35. Ibid. p. 38.

36. Ibid. p. 47.

his demand was *not* justifiable, your further compliance would undoubtedly derive from his exercise of power, not authority. The point is that the policeman's badge, uniform, and gun—his symbols of "formal power"—do not constitute his authority. Whether he actually has that depends upon the authoritativeness of his communication, and that depends to a considerable degree upon the reasonableness of his command.

If the officer's elaboration of his demand to enter was sound in terms of the law, did he not have authority? Within the frame of our example, the answer is both no and yes. No, as far as you were concerned, since the elaboration did not make sense in terms of your own values. Yes, as far as society and its courts are concerned—provided, of course, that they themselves considered the law to be authoritative. As can readily be seen, in this kind of situation—which occurs frequently—authority is both a source of and a restraint upon the exercise of power; it both justifies and limits the use of power. To those who believe in democracy this affords small comfort, unless authority itself is grounded upon reasoning that is meaningful to a majority of the people.

As a final note, it is worth observing that just as authority can be transformed into power, so can the reverse obtain. "Brainwashing" after the manner of George Orwell's "Big Brother" (and his real-life counterpart in Communist China) is a gruesome case in point. To obey Big Brother is not enough; you must *love* him. A different kind of illustration of the same point is the parent who uses the threat of spanking (power) to produce filial discipline which is based on acceptance of certain rules of the game (authority). Authority, in short, can cut both ways. In a humane and healthy society it can perform the valuable function of limiting the behavior of men, especially those in official positions, to legitimate acts; for their actions must be potentially justified by "reasoned elaboration" in terms of values of a sane

society. However, if the value frame of the society is patho-
logical, authority, even as we have regarded it, can become a
tool in furthering the state of pathology.

V

Perhaps the best way to summarize our effort to draw careful
distinctions among power and related concepts is to apply
them in a "real world" context—say, a Southern community
where white citizens have decided to abide by a federal
court's desegregation order. As should be evident in the ac-
companying table, we assume that different persons in the
community had different reasons for bowing before the law.

Local officials and local businessmen, for example, were
fearful of severe deprivations—they responded to an exercise
of power. Those whites we style as "moderates," on the other
hand, fall into two distinct groups: (a) those (Group I)
who accepted as legitimate and reasonable the *substantive
logic* underlying the Court order, and (b) those (Group II)
who rejected the substantive ground but accepted the *judicial procedure* as legitimate and reasonable. Both groups,
that is, responded to authority, in the vital senses that both
perceived the Court's decree rationally and both considered
it (even though on different grounds) to be capable of "reasoned elaboration."

A third body of whites—whom, following David Riesman,
we label "other-directed"—complied not because they feared
severe deprivations (power) nor because they thought the
order was reasonable and legitimate (authority), but because they felt obliged to follow the lead of those in the community they most respect (influence). Stated differently,
although the "other-directed" group regarded the Court's ruling as illegitimate and unreasonable both on substantive and
procedural grounds, it "went along with its betters."

Like those who were other-directed, the "masses," too, de-

Table I. Hypothetical Behavior of Southern Whites
to a Desegregation Court Order

CONCEPT	SUBJECT
Power	*Groups Which Choose Compliance*
(relational, demand rationally perceived, conflict of values, threat of severe sanctions)	State and local officials (threat of criminal contempt) Businessmen (threat of economic boycott and race strife, resulting in loss of profits)
Authority	
(relational, demand rationally perceived and considered reasonable, possible conflict of values, no severe sanctions)	Moderates I (substantive grounds for Court's ruling reasonable) Moderates II (substantive grounds unreasonable, but judicial process legitimate and reasonable)
Influence	
(relational, demand rationally perceived, conflict of values, no severe sanctions)	"Other-Directed" Persons (judicial ruling, substantively and procedurally unreasonable, but apprehensive of standing in community)
	Groups Which Choose Neither Compliance Nor Noncompliance
	Mass (conform to dominant behavior in community, with little or no recognition of the problem nor awareness of complying)
Manipulation	
(non-relational, non-rational, no conflict of values nor sanctions)	
Force	*Groups Which Choose Noncompliance*
(relational to non-relational, non-rational, application of severe sanctions)	Defiant official subject to contempt of Court (incarceration reflects that values underlying defiance overshadow values gained by compliance)
Power, Authority, etc.	Extreme segregationists

ferred to the newly dominant viewpoint in the community. Unlike the former, the latter did so with little or no awareness of the issues at stake or of the fact that they were reversing their previous stand on the general question. The "masses," in other words, did not make a conscious choice between compliance and noncompliance with the Court order; following the pattern of manipulation, they simply conformed.

Under the heading of groups not complying with the Court order are officials who are incarcerated and fined for criminal contempt (force) and segregationist groups that are beyond the reach of the Court. Suffice it to say that the behavior of these groups—geared as they are to a different set of values—also can be analyzed and categorized in terms of power and its related concepts.

3
Key Concepts:
Decisions and Nondecisions

DECISIONS

For our purposes, a decision is "a set of actions related to and including the choice of one alternative rather than another . . ." [1] or, more simply, "a choice among alternative modes of action . . . ." [2] Thus, we differ sharply from Lasswell and Kaplan, to whom a decision is "a policy involving severe sanctions (deprivations)." [3] The basis for the contrast between our definition and theirs is clear-cut: they hold that decisions are brought about solely by the exercise of power, while we believe that power is neither the only nor even the major factor underlying the process of decision-making. We believe, in fact, that in some situations power is not involved at all, that in such situations the behavior of decision-makers and their subjects alike can be explained

1. Robert A. Dahl, "The Analysis of Influence in Local Communities," in Charles Adrian (ed.) *Social Science and Community Action* (East Lansing, Mich., 1960), p. 26.
2. Peter Rossi, "Community Decision-Making," in Roland Young (ed.) *Approaches to the Study of Politics* (Evanston, Ill., 1958), p. 364.
3. Op. cit. p. 74.

39

partially or entirely in terms of force, influence, or authority.

Our position can be clarified by reference to the following diagram. Two important points may be drawn from it. First, every social decision involves interaction between the one or more persons seeking a given goal and the one or more persons whose compliance must be obtained. Thus, if A's attempt to exercise power or influence over B is ignored, there is no decision.

Second, compliance can be *sought* through the exercise of one or any combination of the four phenomena indicated on the diagram. However, if compliance is forthcoming, *it may or may not stem from the same source.* For instance, if B bows to A's demands because A has threatened sanctions which B wishes to avoid, the resulting decision is one of "pure" power; both participants made their choices in the same frame of reference. On the other hand, if B's compliance is grounded, not on a fear of deprivations but on acceptance of A's values, the resulting decision is a hybrid case, in the important sense that A sought to exercise power, but in fact exercised authority. Similarly, cases can be identified in which A has sought to exert authority while B's compliance was given because he was influenced (see diagram). The combinations are many—particularly if the analysis also takes into account situations where two or more of the phenomena come into play simultaneously.[4] The point is, in all events, that a decision cannot be said to be a result of power or influence or authority or force unless and until it is specified from whose point of view the decision is being examined, that is, from that of the one who seeks compliance or the one who gives it.

4. For example, A may employ both authority and power to gain B's agreement, and B's response may have a similarly dual basis. An apparent case in point is the relationship between Adolf Hitler and some of his military chiefs during World War II. On this, consult William L. Shirer, *The Rise and Fall of the Third Reich* (New York, 1966), pp. 366 ff. and *passim.*

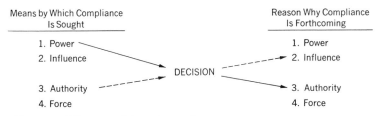

Figure 1. Diagram of impulse and response

It may be objected that this approach is unworkable for empirical analysis because it necessitates mind-reading. We think not. Courts of law distinguish between "specific" intent and intent inferred from actual behavior, and so can we. In other words, we believe, that it is both feasible and necessary to deduce from detailed observation of the situation why persons act as they do.[5] To put it still another way, there is no short-cut, no simple and mechanical method for gaining a full understanding of the decision-making process.

We concede that our approach is less workable than that of Lasswell and Kaplan, Dahl, and others of that "school." On the other hand, because ours provides a broader conceptual frame within which to analyze decision-making, it makes easier the comparative study of the factors underlying different decisions in diverse circumstances. A road is thereby opened toward the development of a body of general theory with respect to the decision-making process. Moreover, because we distinguish carefully among the forces at work in any given situation, we minimize the risk of putting unwarranted emphasis upon one factor to the exclusion, wholly or partly, of others. Stated more bluntly, we put the phenomenon of power in proper perspective: we recognize

5. The approach we have in mind is exemplified by the comparatively unstructured, but nonetheless penetrating, study of "Springdale" by Joseph Vidich and Arthur Bensman, *Small Town in Mass Society* (Princeton, N.J., 1958). For further discussion of this point, see following section.

that while decision-making frequently does involve power relationships, it very often does not.

Policy choices are frequently made in the absence of a clear-
cut, once-for-all decision. They simply "happen," in the
sense that certain steps are taken that are necessary but preliminary to a decision, and the sequence of steps acquires (as
the saying goes) a life of its own. There is reliable evidence,
for instance, that President Truman's "decision" to order an
atomic attack on Hiroshima in August 1945 was totally fore-
ordained: although he and his top advisers were debating
the pros and cons of the policy choice to the last moment,
the technical arrangements for the attack were so complete
that a decision to call it off was all but impossible.[6] Similarly, it appears that by the time President Kennedy was
faced with a decision on the Bay of Pigs venture in 1961, the
preparations had progressed to a point that virtually foreclosed all options but one.[7]

What Braybrooke and Lindblom label disjointed incrementalism is closely analogous to what we label decision-less
decisions.[8] Paraphrased loosely, disjointed incrementalism is
the process of making policy choices by means of a sequence
of steps, each of which effects a small change at the margin.
The continuous alteration over the years in the structure of
individual and corporation income taxes is a case in point. A
chief justification for incremental decision-making is, of
course, that it permits the leadership to proceed toward
amelioration of a problem in small steps, testing and correct-

6. Len Giovanitti and Freed, *The Decision to Drop the Atomic Bomb* (New
York, 1962).
7. Arthur M. Schlesinger, Jr., *A Thousand Days* (New York, 1965), Ch. X.
8. David Braybrooke and C. E. Lindblom, *A Strategy of Decision* (New York,
1963), Ch. 5.

ing for errors or difficulties as they go. The process may, however, have undesired results: rational, conscious, and incremental decisions a, b, c, and d may give rise to a major qualitative change that was unforeseen, a change that was wholly or substantially unintended, that is, a decision-less decision. Once again, the fiasco in the Bay of Pigs may be cited for illustration.

Incremental decision-making can be both unwitting and deliberate. Thus, if A's policy conflicts with that of B, and A makes repeated adjustments at the margin to overcome B's objections to A's policy, the latter will at some point become transformed into something quite different from what was originally intended. As an example, President Kennedy's chief interest in 1963 was the reform of the income-tax structure and, only secondarily, a general tax-rate reduction. To get the necessary votes in Congress, however, he and his successor made repeated concessions until the bill that eventually was passed provided some reduction in the level of tax rates but no significant structural reforms.

In any event, when incrementalism does produce a major policy change, the political analyst must take care not to assign full responsibility for the change to those who participated in the last few incremental choices.

NONDECISIONS

Political systems and sub-systems develop a "mobilization of bias," [9] a set of predominant values, beliefs, rituals, and institutional procedures ("rules of the game") that operate systematically and consistently to the benefit of certain persons and groups at the expense of others. Those who benefit are placed in a preferred position to defend and promote their vested interests. More often than not, the "status-quo defenders" are a minority or elite group within the popula-

9. E. E. Schattschneider, *The Semi-Sovereign People* (New York, 1960), p. 71.

tion in question. Elitism, however, is neither foreordained nor omnipresent: as opponents of the war in Viet Nam can readily attest, the mobilization of bias can and frequently does benefit a clear majority.

The primary method for sustaining a given mobilization of bias is nondecision-making. A nondecision, as we define it, is a decision that results in suppression or thwarting of a latent or manifest challenge to the values or interests of the decision-maker. To be more nearly explicit, nondecision-making is a means by which demands for change in the existing allocation of benefits and privileges in the community can be suffocated before they are even voiced; or kept covert; or killed before they gain access to the relevant decision-making arena; or, failing all these things, maimed or destroyed in the decision-implementing stage of the policy process.[10]

Nondecision-making can take any of several forms. The most direct and extreme form is one in which force is invoked as the means of preventing demands for change in the established order from entering the political process. A case in point is white terrorization—harassment, imprisonment, beatings, even murder—of civil-rights workers in the rural South.

Just as direct but less extreme is nondecision-making through exercise of power. The threat of sanctions against the initiator of a potentially threatening demand may be negative or positive, ranging from intimidation (potential deprivation of valued things or events) to cooptation (potential rewards). A particularly potent form of cooptation is "participatory democracy": in Philip Selznick's words, it

10. For a critical analysis of the concept of nondecision-making, see Richard M. Merelman, "On the Neo-Elitist Critique of Community Power," *American Political Science Review*, LXII (June 1968), pp. 451–61; and Raymond E. Wolfinger, "Community Power and Policy Making in American Cities" (forthcoming). Our brief comment on Merelman, together with his reply, may be found in *American Political Science Review*, LXII (December 1968), pp. 1268–69.

gives "the opposition the illusion of a voice without the voice itself, and so stifles opposition without having to alter policy in the least." [11] Would-be initiators of change can also be deterred by reminders from the status-quo defender that illegitimate sanctions—for example, denial of bank credit, dismissal from employment, revocation of draft deferment, etc.—can be invoked if the prevailing allocation of values continues to be called seriously into question.

A third and indirect form of nondecision-making is one that invokes an existing bias of the political system—a norm, precedent, rule or procedure—to squelch a threatening demand or incipient issue. For example, a demand for change may be denied legitimacy by being branded socialistic, unpatriotic, immoral, or in violation of an established rule or procedure. Challenges can also be deflected by referring the demands or issues to committees or commissions for detailed and prolonged study or by steering them through time-consuming and ritualistic routines that are built into the political system. Tactics such as these, which are highly effective means "to screen out any energetic search for innovation," [12] are particularly effective when employed against impermanent or weakly organized groups (e.g. students, the poor), which have difficulty withstanding delay.[13] Yet another effective ploy is the use of symbolic appeals, based upon norms of the system, in order to distort or transform a threatening demand into an innocuous one.[14]

The fourth and most indirect form of nondecision-making

11. Quoted in James S. Coleman, *Community Conflict* (New York, 1957), p. 17.
12. Ibid. p. 54.
13. Michael Lipsky, "Protest as a Political Resource," *American Political Science Review*, LXII (December 1968), p. 1156. Upon occasion, referral to committees or commissions backfires, in that the study group's report feeds the flames of dissent. The Report of the National Advisory Commission on Civil Disorders (Kerner Commission) in 1968 probably had this effect.
14. For illustrations of this point, see Murray Edelman, *The Symbolic Uses of Power* (Urbana, Ill., 1967).

involves reshaping or strengthening the mobilization of bias in order to block challenges to the prevailing allocation of values. As an illustration, the university administration may establish additional rules and procedures for processing students' demands for change. Another tactic is to reinforce existing barriers, or construct new ones, against challengers' efforts to widen the scope of conflict. For example, the demands of rent-strikers can be blunted or dulled by insisting that tenant-landlord relations are a purely private matter. Similarly, the dominance of great corporations over small ones is fortified by "privatization of conflict," [15] rationalized by reference to imperatives of the free-enterprise system.

We must take note of one more kind of situation which is closely allied to, but actually is not nondecision-making in the strict sense. The reference is to situations where B, confronted by A who has greater power resources, decides not to make a demand upon A for fear that the latter will invoke sanctions against him. Although B's course of action makes it appear that A has made a nondecision, all that can be said is that A "possessed" power in a nondecision form and B reacted to it.[16]

Our critics, especially Professors Merelman and Wolfinger, have made much of the point that B's non-action, based upon his anticipation of A's reaction, is a "non-event" which is, by nature, impossible of empirical verification.[17] We concede the point, but vigorously deny their broader contention that *all* nondecisions are non-events. To put it affirmatively, although absence of conflict may be a non-event, a decision which results in prevention of conflict *is* very much an event —and an observable one to boot.

15. Grant McConnell, *Private Power and American Democracy* (New York. 1966), pp. 91–118.
16. This formulation accords with that of Robert A. Dahl, "Power," in *International Encyclopedia of the Social Sciences* (New York, 1968), Vol. XII.
17. See footnote 10 above.

EMPIRICAL IDENTIFICATION OF NONDECISIONS

How does an investigator identify a nondecision? Direct questioning of those concerned will be to little avail. Nondecision-makers themselves are often not aware of the full implications of what they have done, and even when they are, they probably will be at some pains to conceal their intentions and purposes. By the same token, those who are adversely affected either do not understand the process by which they were disarmed or are so preoccupied with their defeat that they have little interest in how it was effected.

The appropriate place for the investigator to begin is with the process of decision-making. Specifically, by exploring a set of concrete decisions which have been taken in the community, he will accumulate a list of individuals and groups who participated, either openly or behind the scenes, in the process of conflict resolution. Beyond that, his detailed study of the decision-making process will yield valuable clues about the prevailing mobilization of bias, as it is reflected in the rituals and rules of the game operative in the decision-making institutions. Most importantly of all, he will gain insights as to (a) which persons and groups are short-changed or disfavored as a result of the mobilization of bias and (b) whether and to what extent their interests are expressed in the political system.

It goes almost without saying that the actual decisions to be studied must involve issues that are important to those concerned. Certain contests are "lost" by those who are more powerful, more authoritative or more influential than their adversaries, simply because the apparent losers consider the issue inconsequential and not worth expenditure of their (finite) resources. What, then, constitutes an "important" or "key" issue? A key issue, in our terms, is one that involves a genuine challenge to the resources of power or authority of

those who currently dominate the process by which policy
outputs in the system are determined. Stated differently, a
key issue is one that involves a demand for enduring trans-
formation in both the manner in which values are allocated
in the polity in question and the value-allocation itself. Conceptually speaking, there is a fundamental difference between a heated controversy over, say, fair housing and one
involving transfer of power or authority with respect to allocation of anti-poverty funds from affluent whites to impoverished blacks. The former issue may be a "one-shot" affair,
having no bearing upon the capacity of the poor to effect
continuing change in the nature of policy outputs. It is that
capacity, on a sustained basis, which constitutes a significant
exercise of power or authority.

To distinguish in this way between key and relatively unimportant issues is conceptually, but not empirically tenable.
In many circumstances what appears to be a one-shot issue
proves in retrospect to have been only the beginning of a sustained power-authority conflict. As a consequence, empirical
determination of whether an issue is important or unimportant is not possible until such time as the investigator has ac-
quired detailed knowledge about the mobilization of bias
and the nondecision-making process. And that knowledge
cannot be fully developed until *after* close scrutiny of a number of key decisions. In the jargon of the critical-path analysts, we seem to be caught in a loop.

There is a way out of the difficulty. Several decisions that
appear to involve key issues may be studied. Clues emanating therefrom may then be pursued, as outlined above, in
order to gain an understanding of the mobilization of bias.
Not until the last step, exploration of nondecision-making,
would a judgment be passed on whether a given issue was
important.

The question remains, How can an outside observer determine if and how the prevailing mobilization of bias is

buttressed by nondecisions? Armed with the leads picked up from his study of the decision-making process, he must determine if those persons and groups apparently disfavored by the mobilization of bias have grievances, overt or covert. Both types are easily ascertainable; the only difference between them, by our definition, is that overt grievances are those that have already been expressed and have generated an issue within the political system, whereas covert ones are still *outside* the system. The latter, that is, are covert in the sense that they have not been recognized as "worthy" of public attention and controversy, but they are overt in that they are observable in their aborted form to the investigator.

The observer may find that no one is aggrieved in the community. In that event, he would be ill-advised to search for evidence of nondecision-making. If there is no conflict, overt or covert, the presumption must be that there is consensus on the prevailing allocation of values, in which case nondecision-making is impossible. However, if grievances there are, the investigator's next step is to determine why and by what means some or all of the potential demands for change have been denied an airing. Which of change-seekers' complaints, he must ask, were denied access to an arena of conflict, which were branded as violative of predominant values and therefore nullified, and which were sidetracked and eventually squashed by referral to a hostile committee or other dilatory tactics?

Suppose the observer can uncover no grievances, no actual or potential demands for change. Suppose, in other words, there appears to be universal acquiescence in the status quo. Is it possible, in such circumstances, to determine empirically whether the consensus is genuine or instead has been enforced through nondecision-making? The answer must be negative. Analysis of this problem is beyond the reach of a political analyst and perhaps can only be fruitfully analyzed by a philosopher. Put more forcibly, in the absence of con-

flict—a power struggle, if you will—there is no way accurately
to judge whether the thrust of a decision really is to thwart
or prevent serious consideration of a demand for change that
is potentially threatening to the decision-maker.

For purposes of analysis, a power struggle exists, overtly or
covertly, either when both sets of contestants are aware of its
existence or when only the less powerful party is aware of it.
The latter case is relevant where the domination of status-
quo defenders is so secure and pervasive that they are obli-
vious of any persons or groups desirous of challenging their
pre-eminence. Unawareness of potential challengers does not
mean, however, that the dominant group will refrain from
making nondecisions that protect or promote their dominance. Simply supporting the established political process
tends to have this effect. In plain language, as students of
power and its consequences, our main concern is not
whether the defenders of the status quo use their power consciously, but rather if and how they exercise it and what effects it has on the political process and other actors within
the system. Within the context of an identifiable power
struggle, the analyst is in a position to observe the extent to
which power is exercised and its effectiveness in preventing
an issue from being raised, or, if raised, aborted before it
reaches the decision-making arena.

Application of the above procedure to an analysis of community power, authority and influence will provide valuable
clues about who rules, an elite or elites or the many, but that
is not its main contribution. In fact, our approach tends to
reverse the basic question. Rather than asking, Who rules? it
asks, What persons or groups in the community are especially
disfavored under the existing distribution of benefits and
privileges? It asks, further, To what extent does the utilization of power, authority and influence shape and maintain a
political system that tends to perpetuate "unfair shares" in
the allocation of values; and how, if at all, are new sources of

power, authority, and influence generated and brought to bear in an effort to alter the political process and in turn lessen inequality in the value allocation?

In providing a broader focus for observing the use of power and its correlates as they interact with ideology and political institutions, we gain a clearer understanding of the political behavior of individuals and groups who have a common interest in shaping, sustaining, and benefiting from a favorable bias in the system. Moreover, the broader focus opens hitherto-unexplored avenues for study of the power relationships between those who are favored by the system and those who are at a significant disadvantage.

4

A Model of the Political Process

We are now in a position to discuss our conception or "model" of the political process. As with any model, ours is an abstraction from reality, a schematic depiction of the real world. The test of its validity is not whether it truly mirrors the political system of a *particular* community, but whether it is a useful frame of reference for analysis of the forces that shape and implement major policy changes in *any* community.

It is our belief that the model is useful for analyzing the whole, as well as any part, of a community's political system, defined here as all persons, groups, and institutions—both private and governmental—trying to sustain or alter the existing authoritative allocation of values. Analysis of the system as a whole necessitates investigation of all important conflicts between various alignments of persons, groups, and institutions in the community. This involves, in turn, analysis of each of several mobilizations of bias and of their interrelationships, for example, the biases operative in relationships between the business community and City Council may be quite different from those that operate in the conflict between militant blacks and white decision-makers. Our own empirical work, reported in Chapters 5–7 below, is more limited in scope. Because our main interest was in analyzing political interaction between the black poor in Baltimore and the white-dominated "Establishment," we have used the model to focus on the shaping and implementation of anti-poverty policies and programs. Although our findings extend beyond the focal point, shedding light on other important conflicts in the city, they cannot sustain generalizations about the over-all "power structure" in Baltimore.

The remainder of this chapter is devoted to discussion of the properties of our model, which is depicted schematically in Figure 2.

PERSONS AND GROUPS
SEEKING REALLOCATION OF VALUES

The category "persons and groups seeking reallocation of values" (upper left-hand corner of the diagram) encompasses: (a) individuals and associations (in federal, state, and city government, organized religion, education, politics, mass communication, philanthropy, civic improvement) who have manifested a substantial interest in changing the broad outlines of anti-poverty policy and have some capacity to exercise power and its correlates in order to achieve their objectives; (b) associations actively promoting specific interests, such as civil rights (NAACP, CORE), white supremacy (KKK, American Nazi party), tax relief (tax-payers' associations), commercial and industrial development (Chamber of Commerce), social welfare (settlement houses), social work associations; and (c) latent and potential groups (e.g. the poverty population) who are currently uninterested in the policy-making process or are powerless, but who are likely in the future to become active and capable of exercising power and its correlates within the political system.[1]

1. For a discussion of the differences among pressure groups, see E. E. Schatt-schneider, *The Semi-Sovereign People* (New York. 1960), Ch. II.

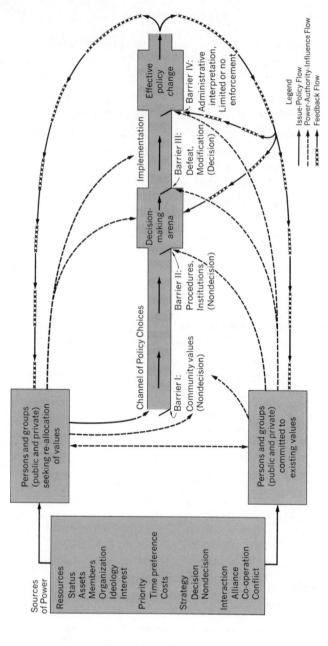

Figure 2. The Political System: Flow of Anti-poverty Power

At the outset, the analyst is confronted with the problems of identifying the individuals and groups under sub-classes (a) and (b) [2] and of analyzing the power-authority-influence resources available to each unit for use in achieving desired changes in policy. Specifically, the problem is one of appraising in each case the relationships among the following variables: kind and magnitude of resources available to the person or group; priority ranking of the unit's immediate policy objective in relation to its other goals; its willingness to expend the necessary resources; and the soundness of its strategy for gaining its objective.

The resources of an individual or organization include, in addition to its financial capacity, the magnitude of its operation and the degree of dependency of the community upon it, the size and leadership-control of its constituency, its status in the eyes of the community, and its ideology. Clearly, if a group has high status (a university in contrast to the Teamsters' Union) and its ideology (political philosophy) is in harmony with community values, it has, all other things being equal, a greater opportunity than a less prestigious organization to translate its demands into authoritative terms and to have ready access to decision-makers. The ideology of an organization is also important in appraising its potentiality to co-operate with other change-seeking groups in a common cause. The long-range interests of NAACP and CORE have been approximately the same, but if their ideological differences grow, the likelihood of their working together to achieve common objectives will be diminished and their separate and joint effectiveness in bringing about change accordingly impaired.

As we have indicated, there can be an immense gap between the *availability* of resources of power-authority-influence and the exercise of power-authority-influence for pur-

2. An analysis of (c) must wait until the entire political process has been examined. See section on feedback, pp. 62–63.

poses of achieving a given goal. To a large extent, the gap is explainable by the priority ranking of the goal, the willingness of the decision-maker(s) to commit scarce resources to attain an objective and his (their) appraisal of the cost in resources to achieve it. If the priority ranking of a goal in relationship to other objectives is high, but costs of goal-seeking are also expected to be high and realization of the goal is not a matter of urgency, it can be reliably predicted that utilization of resources will be low in relation to their magnitude.

PERSONS AND GROUPS
COMMITTED TO EXISTING VALUES

In all respects save one, the actors in this category are similar to those seeking a reallocation of values. The single difference is that the opponents of change have in varying degrees a stake in the maintenance of prevailing policy and are either active or potential supporters of ongoing programs. This is not to say that every unit which defends established policy is politically conservative. For that matter, neither is it true that every unit seeking reallocation of values is radical or even liberal. In terms of the liberal-conservative distinction, each class of units contains a mixture of policy preferences. It is conceivable, for example, that the John Birch Society and the Socialist Workers' party might make common cause for the emasculation of an anti-poverty program. It is equally conceivable that a civil-rights organization whose members stand to gain from existing policy might, despite a radical ideology, defend the program in its present form against the attacks of a conservatively oriented civil-rights group whose members benefit only slightly from current policy. Interest considerations such as these do not invariably override ideology, but they do to an extent sufficient to make unrealistic a sharp division between classes of persons and associations that is based solely on ideological grounds.

Individuals and groups, both liberal and conservative, who are bent upon maintaining the current allocation of values are likely to focus on preventing demands for a reallocation of values from reaching the decision-making stage, rather than running the risk that hostile demands will not be voted down when they are ripe for decision. For that reason, after completing an analysis of each unit's resources, set of priorities, strategy, and interaction with others, the analyst should concern himself with the degree to which the persons and groups, separately or in various combinations, attempt to reinforce prevailing community values, myths, and beliefs that tend to reaffirm existing anti-poverty policy and therefore stand as a barrier to serious reconsideration of policy (Barrier 1 in the diagram). He should also consider the possibility that "status-quo-oriented" individuals and groups, especially those within the governmental structure, will exert power-authority-influence to create new or to support existing political procedures, customs, and institutions that tend to block "unsafe" issues from reaching the decision-making arena (Barrier 2 in the diagram).

Individuals and groups seeking maintenance of currently predominant values also have the option of directly exercising power—and to a less extent, authority—against persons and associations seeking reallocation of values. For example, it is conceivable that a maintenance-oriented government agency could successfully threaten sanctions against a nongovernmental group seeking change, e.g. "if you persist in your demands, we will decide in favor of the proposal of a rival organization." (The exercise of power in this way would constitute a non-decision, since it would be an attempt to prevent an issue from reaching the decision-making stage.) If, of course, the status-quo defender was unsuccessful and the demand for a policy change persisted, the agency would still be able to oppose it within the decision-making arena or, as a last resort, within the implementation arena.

While advocates of change must win at all stages of the political process—issue-recognition, decision, and implementation of policy—the defenders of existing policy must win at only one stage in the process. It is difficult to avoid the conclusion that all political systems have an inherent "mobilization of bias" and that this bias strongly favors those currently defending the status quo.

CHANNEL OF POLICY CHOICES

The channel of policy choices contains every demand for a policy change that receives public notice and engenders public discussion to the point that the demand becomes an issue that presses for resolution in the decision-making arena.[3] The channel, as is shown in the diagram, is partially closed off by formidable barriers. The first barrier, as was noted earlier, consists of values, beliefs, and myths that the dominant portion of the community embraces. The barrier serves to suppress grievances reflecting values that conflict fundamentally with prevailing norms, and it rejects from serious public consideration those demands which are publicly articulated, but which again are radically at odds with the dominant view of what constitutes a politically legitimate issue. If the demand is not within the scope of legitimacy—for example, a proposal that the federal government use the war on poverty as a means of consciously promoting a social revolution in great cities—it will either receive no serious attention

3. See David Easton, *A Systems Analysis of Political Life* (New York, 1965), p. 121. Easton focuses in his work upon the institutional and cultural mechanisms which regulate the flow of issues into the political system and, in the process, prevent the system from destruction from "demand overload." He gives no consideration to the possibility that the mechanisms operate to protect vested interests in a political system from potential demands from other groups in society.

or will be used to discredit the person or organization that proposed it.

A proposal or issue that is within the community-value scope of legitimacy and is backed by sufficient power, authority, or influence to gain public attention may, but will not necessarily, progress to the gates of Barrier II (see diagram). Status-quo-oriented persons or groups may succeed in branding the issue as illegitimate, e.g. by arguing noisily and at length that the proposal is communistic, socialistic, reactionary. Or they may succeed in shifting the interpretation of prevailing values so as to undermine the legitimacy of the issues; "de-segregation is fine, but laws that forbid racial discrimination in the sale of single-family homes violate the freedom of the homeowner." Finally, the persons and groups seeking to maintain established values can ignore the challenge to their position and concentrate on attempting, by resort to power or force, to silence the issue-initiator.

On the other hand, a demand for change which initially is on the periphery of the existing community-value scope and which is supported by skillful exercise of power, authority, or influence has the potentiality of expanding the public, of generating wider support and thereby altering radically the nature of community values. The shift in public reaction from anti- to pro-unionism during the struggle of organized labor to become recognized in the mid-'thirties is a case in point. The March on Washington in 1963 is another dramatic instance in which a demand for change, skillfully handled and fortified by an impressive show of widespread public support, contributed perceptibly to a change in national values.

The interaction, in other words, between community values and issues is a two-way phenomenon: community values, analogous to the repressive mechanism of the super-ego of the individual, disallow "illegitimate" issues from entering the public consciousness. But once the issues are admitted, the new values have the capacity, under certain conditions, substantially to alter the repressive mechanism.

Issues which withstand attack within the channel of policy choices must still hurdle the barriers that impede entrance to the decision-making arena. These barriers consist of procedures, customs, and organizational devices, typified in the U.S. House of Representatives by the committee-system seniority rule, and by the Rules Committee and Ways and Means Committee themselves. Each legislative system has similar barriers that serve the function of selecting in somewhat disguised fashion from among a welter of competing public demands those issues that key decision-makers are prepared or compelled to consider for decision. Devious roads of access and poor communications channels from certain sectors of the public to decision-makers are not necessarily either accidental or inefficient. Viewed from the standpoint of dominant status-quo-oriented groups, both inside and outside the plenary body, disruption in the communications flow can serve a highly useful function.[4]

THE DECISION-MAKING PROCESS [5]

Issues which survive the ideological and procedural barriers of the political system must be resolved through the process of decision-making. Detailed analysis of this process devolves around four key questions.

The first query is obvious: Who makes the decision or, more generally, what individuals or groups play a significant role in the process? Next, what do the decision-makers believe are the relevant factors and conditions—for example,

4. On this point consult Karl W. Deutsch, *The Nerves of Government* (New York, 1966), Parts II–III.
5. This section draws heavily upon the discussion in Richard C. Snyder, "A Decision-Making Approach," in Roland A. Young (ed.), *Approaches to the Study of Politics* (Evanston, Ill., 1958).

public opinion, reactions of those likely to be affected directly, the ideological milieu in the community—that may affect their choice of a course of action? Third, to what extent were the decision-makers constrained by incomplete or inaccurate information, imperfections in the network of communications linking all those involved, precedents that narrow their range of choice, their own perceptions of the problem in its setting, or the availability of resources to implement the decision? Finally, what were the principal determinants of the actors' behavior? To what extent was each participant's choice in the matter dictated by his sphere of competence (formal functions, ranking in the hierarchy, anticipated reactions), by the established rules as to who communicates with whom, by his viewpoint concerning what goals were sought and why, and by his own personality?

POLICY IMPLEMENTATION

The shaping of policy, as is well known, continues throughout the implementation stage of a formal policy decision. In fact, the forces that propel and impinge upon policy through the bureaucratic process of implementation are not dissimilar from forces which give direction and shape to issues prior to reaching the formal decision-making stage. Both the issue-formation and implementation processes are within the political system and in both areas power, authority, and influence are exercised by groups and individuals within and outside the government. And in both areas barriers in the form of values, procedures, and customs are operative in restricting or reshaping stated policy.

Such is the force of law upon the bureaucracy and its hierarchical structure that it can be expected that the exercise of authority will be a more important factor in the execution of policy than in the issue-formulation and decision-making phases of the political process. However, the discretionary

leeway within this realm and the imperfection of communications (some of which is functional and some dysfunc-
tional) is sufficiently great to allow the bureaucrat to exercise power, authority, and influence—and, in extreme cases,
force—to achieve his policy preferences. Thus, for purposes
of analysis, the issue, decision, and implementation processes can generally be treated in the same way.

FEEDBACK

In the absence of knowledge about the impact of the outputs
of a political system, i.e. actual policy changes, on various
groups and institutions, the political analyst would be severely handicapped in understanding the dynamics of power-authority-influence relations within the system. If, for example, an anti-poverty policy is having the effect of politiciz-
ing the poor, it would be useful to know what reaction that
development has had upon various groups, for instance, civil-rights organizations, politicians, and government agencies.
It might well be that if such a policy were continued, the potential power of the poor would become a reality. But in
light of the existing structure of values, rituals, and procedures in the community would such a policy be allowed to
continue? An answer to this kind of question would, at least
initially, depend upon the extent to which communication
lines existed between the anti-poverty agencies and their
components, on one hand, and various groups throughout
the community, on the other. Obviously, for example, if status-quo-oriented groups are unaware of a policy and its potential impact upon the community, they would hardly be in
a position to exercise power-authority-influence in opposition.
    It goes almost without saying that there are several ways
in which the flow of issues through the channel of policy
choices can, in due course, alter the structure and functioning of the political process. An effective policy choice can re-

sult in the formation of new groups or the destruction of existing ones. It can undermine the currently predominant set of values, beliefs, and myths, as a result of which those who were initially change-seekers find themselves now cast in the role of status-quo defenders. Or an effective policy choice can result in modification of procedures and rituals, thereby easing change-seekers' future access to decision-making arenas and increasing the likelihood that decisions in their favor will be fully implemented. In short, analysis of feedback opens the road to clear recognition of the dynamic aspects of the political process and of the possibility that the system, in reflecting changes in the distribution of authority and power among groups within it, may be in a process of transition.

Part Two

5

Poverty, Race,
and Politics in Baltimore—I

Thirty years before we began our study in Baltimore, the Negro community of that city had been described as "set apart both by law and custom from the rest of the population . . . [It] lives to a very great extent on its own intellectual and social resources. It has its own churches, its own clubs and societies, its own theaters and other places of amusement and, to a measurable extent, its own charitable and civic organizations . . . The Baltimore Negro . . . has been exceedingly slow to take advantage of his rights as a citizen. In 1932 . . . only fifty-six percent of the Negro population voted, as against seventy-six percent of the whites . . . [The] Negro voter permits himself to be used by politicians. Because of this attitude, . . . very few Negroes are elected to public office; very few are rewarded with appointive positions and, consequently, the race is not properly represented in the councils of government." The report from which these assertions were drawn concluded by urging that Negroes make a greater use of the ballot, so that "the organized political strength of the Negro group could be used to bring about the employment of colored persons as librarians, policemen, firemen and in other public services from which now they are excluded." [1]

In all essential details, this description was as valid in 1965 as it was in 1935. To be sure, during the intervening decades a clear majority of the city's white population had come to acknowledge, however grudgingly, that local Negroes were entitled by law to all civil rights—to vote, own property, attend desegregated schools, ride on desegregated common carriers, have equal access to all public accommodations, etc. In 1965, as in 1935, however, there was a vast difference between what the law called for and what was actually the case.

The situation in 1968 was ostensibly different. A coalition of blacks and whites had lately overcome a stubbornly defended effort by City Council to gerrymander voting districts in a manner highly unfavorable to the black population. The city's schools were at least partially desegregated. A Negro headed one of the city's major departments and other Negroes held important elective and appointive offices in the municipal government. A sizable and still-growing number of black persons was employed as "librarians, policemen, firemen and in other public services." Black-led organizations were playing an increasingly significant role in all aspects of community life.

Did blacks' exercise of power, authority or influence play any significant role in bringing about these changes? If so, what were the sources of their power-authority-influence and how were they exercised? To what extent, if at all, did the gains of Negroes result from a change in the pre-existing mo-

1. P. Stewart Macaulay, "A Study of the Negro's Problems," *The Sunday Sun* of Baltimore, Magazine Section, 31 March 1935, pp. 1–2. The article summarizes the findings of a study, titled "The Negro Community in Baltimore," which was sponsored by the Baltimore Urban League and directed by Dr. Ira deA. Reid.

bilization of bias and, if it did, how great is the likelihood that the structure, *modus operandi* and output of the political system will be permanently altered? These and related matters are discussed in what follows.

THE POLITICAL SYSTEM CIRCA 1965

In the middle 1960's, as had been true for decades passed, the white majority in Baltimore thoroughly dominated the city's political system. With the exception of a seat or two in the City Council, all the elective offices of government were filled by whites, as were all the major appointive offices. No less importantly, virtually all of the city's industrial and commercial establishments were owned and managed by whites, many of whom served from time to time on municipal boards and commissions. To complete the picture, whites dominated all the interest groups—businessmen's associations, taxpayers' groups, landlords' associations, trade unions, etc.—with easy access to the key centers of decision-making. All this, despite that by 1965 the black population of the city was estimated at better than 40 per cent of the total (*versus* only 17 per cent in 1935)!

Put a little differently, as late as 1965 the political system in Baltimore was, for all practical purposes, closed to the people in the "dark ghetto," people who made up roughly 80 per cent of the city's poverty population. In areas of vital concern to them—housing, employment, and education—the poor had access neither to existing public agencies nor established arenas of conflict for the redress of their grievances. Public bodies, such as the welfare department, the school board, and the fire, police and civil-service commissions, were designed, not for resolution of conflict, but for delivery of services within a predetermined set of administrative criteria and rules. The channel of communications was one-way, not two-way, *from* the agencies *to* the poor. Indeed, the agencies were a potent instrument for stifling grievances, in that "uncooperative" and "undeserving" clients could be, and probably were, denied service (force) or threatened with its denial (power).

Nor were there other avenues for the poor to air their grievances and gain redress. The poor had no access to the newspapers or radio and TV stations, and the news media apparently saw no point in becoming self-appointed champions of the down-trodden. The same may be said for the two political parties, established private-interest groups (white and black), and voluntary agencies, all of which routinely provided the city's non-poor population a potential channel for expressing complaints and converting them into issues for decision. In short, the white-dominated political system in Baltimore systematically and consistently produced a city-wide distribution of benefits and privileges that was highly unfavorable to the black poor.

Defense and reinforcement of the white-oriented mobilization of bias were accomplished mainly by means of nondecisions, many of them indirect in nature and unconsciously made. For example, in accordance with established practice in the city, the Mayor's appointees to key municipal boards and commissions were almost invariably white "notables" (economic, political, or social) who could be counted upon to defend the status quo. The appointments, which were easily justified on the ground that important public posts should be filled only by the most highly qualified persons, not only denied Negroes participation in the making of important decisions, but also all but foreclosed the possibility that their grievances could be heard. In other words, blacks' isolation from the political system was made more complete and their political apathy fortified through what may be called a sustaining nondecision, that is, one that, in conjunction with similar actions, prevents an overt challenge to the existing political process and the allocation of values it produces.

A more direct case of nondecision-making was the city government's reaction to an announcement from the national office of the Congress of Racial Equality (CORE) that Baltimore had been designated a "target city" during 1966. CORE's declared purpose was to organize Baltimore's black poor in order to build a power base within a major metropolitan area. It overstates only slightly to say that the announcement electrified the city's white population and also a sizable number of middle-income blacks. The then-Mayor, described even by his political foes as "an integrationist long before it became fashionable among white liberals," was galvanized into action, probably to the surprise of the CORE organizers. With both imagination and speed, the Mayor established a set of "task forces," charging them to study the problems of the city's poor and develop proposals for combating the problems. Accompanied by huzzahs from the news media, influential white liberals, and leaders of black-bourgeois groups, the Mayor took care that each of his task forces had a biracial membership with a strong "liberal" flavor.

Whatever his motives, the Mayor made an extremely effective nondecision. Before CORE's organizers stepped off the train in Baltimore, their planned campaign was aborted. Whatever hope they may have had of forming a working alliance with local liberals, black and white, was shattered by successful pre-emptive co-optation on the Mayor's part. The liberals saw little point in working with an "outside" somewhat-radical group, when their ends could be at least as well pursued through established and respectable channels. CORE thus found itself without access to the political system and with no resources, other than the inert mass of impoverished Negroes, for the exercise of power.

The Mayor achieved two other things. First, by the device

of his task forces, he effectively, even if temporarily, prevented CORE's threatening challenge to the mobilization of bias from entering the channel of policy choices. Second, he framed the issue in terms much different from those of CORE. The central question, as CORE saw it, was: How can the distribution of power in the city be radically changed in order thereby to increase the black poor's share of benefits and privileges? In the Mayor's view the issue was: What and how much can be done *for* the poor, within the established socio-political order? By creating the task forces, the Mayor thus seized the ideological initiative and, in so doing, carried the day.

Business leaders in Baltimore also engaged in nondecision-making. By far the most weighty group of them was the Greater Baltimore Committee (GBC), an association of approximately 100 key figures in local industry and commerce. Organized in the middle 1950's and frankly patterned after Pittsburgh's famed Allegheny Conference, the GBC had compiled by 1965 an impressive record of achievement. Largely through its initiative and continuing effort, the once-shabby and depressed central business district of Baltimore had been transformed into the architecturally handsome, prosperous Charles Center. GBC was also busily engaged in research and planning in the fields of housing, education, and transportation. And one of its offshoots, the Voluntary Council, was laboring to eliminate racial discrimination in employment.

GBC's first decade of achievement won for it a nearly unanimous local reputation as an imaginative, aggressive, and progressive "do-er." Even activists in the black population, including key figures in CORE, the Student Non-Violent Coordinating Committee (SNCC), and the Union for Jobs or Income Now (U-JOIN), openly acknowledged at the time (1965–66) that GBC was doing the "right" things and doing them well. In fact, the forceful leader of U-JOIN was so taken by the Committee and what it appeared to stand for that he submitted to its executive director a position paper, recommending an "alliance between the poor and the power structure."

The author of this proposal soon learned that GBC was not interested in sharing its power, authority, and influence. The Committee's thrust was to improve the *absolute* well-being of the city's entire population, not to effect a redistribution of values in favor of the poverty-stricken blacks. It was, in other words, deflecting potentially threatening challenges to the prevailing mobilization of bias by doing things *for* the poor but not in concert *with* them. By the same token, its warm support for the cause of racial integration amounted to a nondecision in that it helped sustain the ideological breach between the "bourgeois" and the militant blacks, thereby further weakening the political leverage of the latter.[2]

It is important to note that suppression of Negro grievances, although carried out by partially overlapping political and economic elites, was strongly supported by a clear majority of the white population. City councilmen from districts with a predominance of lower-middle-income whites openly espoused racist views and were regularly rewarded with re-election. Equally, voters in the more affluent districts consistently returned councilmen who, though more subtle in their anti-Negro bias, could be counted upon to preserve the status quo.[3]

The grievances of the poverty-stricken blacks, as a result,

2. For purposes of this paper, a black militant is a political activist whose primary objective is the acquisition of sources of political power for the masses of urban black people in the ghettoes. The militant views political conflict as a valued means to build a power base, while the black moderate, although concerned with power, is content to see it exhibited through representatives elected or appointed into the system.

3. See Ronnie Goldberg, "The Politics of Local Government in Baltimore," Appendix A.

remained largely covert. Indeed, the only firm evidence that they had grievances was that upon occasion they would seek access to the political system through the electoral process. Their discontent was also manifested by feeble and abortive efforts on the part of their self-appointed spokesmen to "build a power base," to "get a piece of the action," and to "control policies affecting the black community." As of 1965, in short, the black poor were literally powerless to get their demands into the channel of policy choices, much less to participate actively in the formulation of policies with significant consequences for them.

THE BLACK STRUGGLE FOR POLITICAL ACCESS, 1966–68

Within a year the situation had changed significantly—or so it seemed. Throughout 1966 a coalition of disparate groups, drawn from both races and including all shades of ideology from "moderate" to "radical," had labored to overturn a City Council-backed reapportionment plan for the city and replace it with a scheme more likely to increase the number of black Councilmen. The advance odds against the success of the effort were very high. Not only did the Council majority control the machinery through which reapportionment had to be accomplished, but by denying the Community Action Agency (a department of city government) the right to mount a voter-registration drive, the Council had gone far to assure that comparatively few Negroes were eligible to vote in any referendum on the issue. In the face of these and other obstacles, the anti-Council coalition not only forced a general referendum in November 1966 but won approval for its plan from a clear majority of those voting.[4]

Hard on the heels of this victory, the City Council voted

4. The fight over reapportionment is described in Brenda L. Davies, "The Politics of Reapportionment in Baltimore," Appendix B.

approval of two long-stalled proposals of great interest to Baltimore's poverty population, a self-help housing program and increased rental allowances for welfare recipients. It is impossible to judge whether or to what extent this outcome stemmed from the referendum returns. It remains, however, that the deciding votes in the Council were cast by two members with a previous history of opposition to anti-poverty programs.

Buoyed by these events, black leaders and their supporters confidently expected that in the municipal elections in 1966 their nominees would capture the presidency of City Council and at least four more Councilmanic seats. Their optimism proved to be misplaced. Their candidate for the Council presidency was defeated in the Democratic primary and only two, not four, Negroes won seats in the Council.[5]

The poor showing of black candidates stemmed from several causes. In the first place, despite an extensive voter-registration drive (organized and carried out by a coalition of white and black organizations) prior to the reapportionment referendum, only 22 per cent of eligible black voters were on the voter lists. Second, a significant minority of Negro voters were registered Republicans and therefore could not vote in the Democratic primary. (For many years Negroes were forbidden to participate actively in Democratic politics in Baltimore.) What is more, many black Democrats abstained from voting in their party's primary. Third, in both the primary and general elections of 1967 there were districts with two or more black candidates, backed by feuding black political groups. Negro voting strength was thus diffused. Finally, there was a tendency among black voters in the general election to vote the top of the ticket, ignoring the less important offices.

5. The details in this paragraph and the next are drawn from electoral analyses prepared by Professor Robert D. Loewy of Goucher College. See also Ronnie Goldberg, op. cit.

Another route by which black militants sought during
1966–67 to acquire power and gain access to the political system was organizing their "constituents" around long-standing but hitherto covert grievances. In this area of endeavor
the activists had an open field: neither the two then-incum-
bent black Councilmen nor the local chapter of the NAACP
nor the black-owned and -operated newspaper (the Baltimore
Afro-American) had yet concerned themselves seriously with
the problems of the black poor. The last-named, if organized
successfully, were sufficiently numerous to be a major source
of power. Beyond that, their disadvantages were so many, so
deep-seated, and so clearly incompatible with the popular
conception of distributive justice that demands for their redress could not be ignored indefinitely.

The organizers—initially, U-JOIN, later joined by CORE
and SNCC—took as their tactical premise that the poor must
be induced to participate in protests about specific grievances, such as substandard housing, low-quality education,
unemployment, and racial discrimination. The organizers'
self-determined functions were to shape demands from these
grievances and also to create combative situations in which
the poor, out of anger and a hope of achievement, would actively join the battle. To these ends they promoted demonstrations, mass picketing, strikes, and boycotts.

It must be emphasized that the goal of organization was
not to gain concessions from "The Establishment," but to
build a political base from which assaults could be made
upon the prevailing mobilization of bias. The aim, in other
words, was to overturn—or at least, significantly alter—the
prevailing mobilization of bias. To this end and by the
aforementioned means, the militants labored throughout
1966 and 1967. The rewards were meager by almost any
standard: a few concessions were wrung from the Establishment, and several previously covert grievances were made
overt; but far from having built a solid political base, U-

JOIN, CORE, and SNCC were reduced at the end of 1967 to little more than paper organizations, each consisting of an organizer or two and a literal handful of loyal workers. To be explicit, the black militants focused mainly on three of their constituents' latent or covert grievances. One had to do with the amount and manner of distribution of welfare payments. Under the auspices of U-JOIN, a group of welfare recipients was formed under the label Rescuers from Poverty, in order to provoke confrontations with local and state officials directly concerned with the welfare program. A second group, styling themselves Tenants for Justice in Housing, attempted to bring about improvements in rental-housing quality by means of rent strikes and initiation of legal proceedings against "slumlords." [6] Third, in the name of equal access of blacks and whites to all public accommodations, the black activists organized picketing of local bars known to discriminate against would-be Negro patrons.

On the last-mentioned issue, a limited victory was won, in that the liquor-control board (at the urging of the Mayor and over the objections of a majority of the City Council) compelled its licensees to accede to the blacks' demands. It seems clear, in retrospect, that the blacks won their tactical objective by (a) widening the scope of the conflict beyond just themselves and the bar-owners; (b) exercising authority through the Mayor, who shared their values on this specific issue; and (c) employing a limited amount of force (the picket line), which carried the threat of more severe sanctions (power) in the form of street riots. So far as the black organizers were concerned, there was no savor to this victory. By their frank admission, in private, the bar issue was unimportant both to them and the great majority of those they sought to activate; not only did the city have more than enough bars where Negroes were welcome, but most black

6. James D. Dilts, "Organization Man for the Other America," *The Baltimore Sun*, Magazine Section, 16 June 1968.

citizens preferred watering places close to their homes. What
the militants *really* wanted—a fighting organization—was denied them because the Mayor's quick action both deprived
the militants of their organizing lever and, as a close corollary, reassured the many "moderate" blacks that they could
get much of what they wanted by going along with, rather
than trying to alter the established political order.

The exertions of the Rescuers from Poverty and the Tenants for Justice in Housing yielded neither fighting organizations nor political concessions. Though both groups tried to
widen the scope of conflict on their respective issues, no one
with any weight in the political system was cowed by their
threats nor agreed with their positions: the welfare program
had become noxious to most white taxpayers; and rent
strikes seemed to many whites a potentially dangerous invasion of property rights. Nor were the Rescuers and Tenants
able to enlist the active support of any sizable number of
their black brethren. The latter remained on the sidelines,
whether out of fear of reprisals from social workers and landlords, or of disinterest or apathy or even hostility. So, lacking sufficient power, authority, and influence, a lack reinforced by blacks' virtual exclusion from the political process,
the militants and their small band of followers achieved neither their tactical nor their strategic objective.

Hindsight helps us to see additional reasons for the militants' inability to build an organizational base through promotion of conflict. A main one, adverted to above, is that as
late as the winter of 1967–68 a great many, probably a clear
majority, of Baltimore's Negroes wanted to *avoid* conflict.
This seemed especially true of older persons, those above 30
or 35 years. Some—we cannot say how many—still clung to
the belief that American society was moving toward racial
integration and that the appropriate course for blacks was
moderation and reasonableness. Persons in this category
were distrustful, if not fearful, of those who preached "black

power" or any of its variants. Others—again the total number is unknown—were resigned to their oppressed and depressed lot in life. Each new injury to their economic, social, or political well-being was seen as further confirmation that their exclusion from the political process was complete and everlasting. To describe these individuals as apathetic is to understate. In the apt contemporary phrase, they were "turned off." And together with the "integrationists," they were barren ground for the organizers' seeds.

The would-be organizers had other obstacles to overcome. For one thing, in the inner city as well as elsewhere, it is very difficult to hold together over time a group assembled originally to fight for or against a specific issue. Once the conflict has been resolved, the group tends to disintegrate. Furthermore, inner-city dwellers tend, on average, to change their residences frequently, making it difficult for organizers to keep in touch with them. As an important corollary, highly mobile persons have no sense of belonging to groups within given geographical areas, therefore have little incentive to participate in group activities in their current area of residence.

To summarize, throughout 1966 and 1967 the central political issue for black leaders in Baltimore was how to build an organizational base as a source of power, with which in turn they could gain access to the political process in the city. This two-pronged effort failed. Their success in the reapportionment fight could not be translated into additional seats in City Council, largely because they could not weld a durable coalition among black groups. Their effort to transform the covert grievances of the black population into issues was also abortive, in part because they lacked arenas where they could practice the politics of conflict as distinct from the politics of confrontation,[7] and in part because they

7. ". . . 'confrontation' [refers] to such forms of direct action as deliberate disruption of or interference with normal, routine operations of persons or

had no access to key centers of decision-making. In short, the prevailing mobilization of bias blocked black leaders' attempts to arouse their would-be constituents to political action and thereby assured that blacks would remain "locked out" of the political system.

Nondecisions on behalf of the white majority in the city reinforced the bias against the black poor. The latter's potential adversaries—landlords, employers, bureaucrats, politicians—often found it in their own interest to avoid being drawn into conflict, relying instead for protection of their interests upon established institutions and procedures. Why, for example, should a landlord engage in conflict with his tenants, when the police and courts are prepared to act on his behalf and when the City Council ignores appeals by the poor for a change in the law? By the same token, covert and overt grievances against the system were suffocated in their incipiency, whether because their legitimacy was denied or because they were referred to unsympathetic study commissions, or because they were deflated by grants of politically insignificant concessions.

In early 1968, despite more than two years of increasing effort on their behalf, the black poor in Baltimore were still excluded from the political process. The future prospects looked no less bleak.

institutions by large masses of persons; deliberate violations of authoritative orders [sic] to disperse; . . . the use of ridicule, rudeness, obscenity, and other uncivil forms of speech and behavior to shock, embarrass, or defy authorities; refused to comply with orders or to accept authoritative commands (sic) or requests as legitimate." (Jerome H. Skolnick, *The Politics of Protest*, New York, 1969, p. 106.)

6
Poverty, Race,
and Politics in Baltimore—II

The city of Baltimore was an early enlistee in the "war on poverty" that was declared in 1964 by the President and Congress. The enabling legislation was enacted in August of that year, and the city's Community Action Program was formally established just six months later, February 1965. Ninety per cent financed with federal funds and designated by the Mayor and City Council as Baltimore's "point of fire" in the anti-poverty effort, the Community Action Agency was —at least on paper—an eminently suitable vehicle for the confrontation politics of black organizers. Throughout 1965–67, however, the CAA was all but ignored by the militants and itself accorded low priority to community-organization and citizen-participation activities. Why was this so?

The answer derives in large part from decisions arrived at prior to CAA's creation.[1] For some time before passage of the Economic Opportunity Act of 1964, a coalition of pri-

1. The next six paragraphs are based upon Morton S. Baratz, "The Community Action Program in Baltimore," Appendix D.

81

vate welfare agencies, financed in part by the municipal government, had been engaged in the design of a program of "human renewal," along lines originally laid down under the Gray Areas program of the Ford Foundation. The major inarticulate premise of the Baltimore anti-poverty planners was that first priority in an expanded anti-poverty effort should be given to the filling of gaps in the existing array of welfare services. On that premise they had identified more than two dozen specific programs which would and should be instituted as soon as funds became available. To a very considerable extent, this shopping list formed the basis of Baltimore's subsequent application to the federal government for CAP funds. Significantly, neither the original Plan for Action (as it was called) nor the CAP application had much to say about community organization and its potential role in the anti-poverty effort.

No less importantly, the designers of the Community Action Program concluded that the administering agency had to be part and parcel of the municipal government. Understandably, there is virtually no written evidence of how and why this conclusion was reached. Participants in the debate later told us, however, that they were left no room for doubt that City Council would refuse to appropriate its 10 per cent share of total expenses unless the CAA were a municipal department and thus under Council's direct oversight.

In yet another way was the fledgling CAA constrained from becoming a conflict arena accessible to militant black organizers. The Community Action Commission, charged with formulating policy for the CAP, not only had a minority of black members, but the predetermined qualifications for appointees to the Commission virtually assured exclusion of blacks with a politically martial bent. In plainer language, the criteria for appointment were loaded heavily in favor of "moderates" as opposed to "radicals."

The predictable upshot was that the CAA was closely confined to delivery of services to its target population. An early attempt to allocate some of its resources to a voter-registration drive amongst the poverty population was quickly vetoed by the City Council. The staff of the agency was expressly forbidden to use the neighborhood development centers as focal points for organizing residents for "political action" and also expressly forbidden to take part, individually or collectively, in demonstrations, protest marches, and the like. In short, the Council majority—and by extension, its white supporters in the city—made eminently clear that they would not countenance the use of CAP funds for activities that challenged the prevailing mobilization of bias. Small wonder that the militant blacks scorned the CAP and turned their organizing efforts in other directions.

Although CAA was kept on a short leash, it could not be wholly prevented from moving into the proscribed area. Its main channel of entry thereto was the neighborhood development centers. From the very beginning the anti-poverty planners had conceived of the centers as a new, more effective means for delivering welfare services to the poor. Not only that, the centers were to "involve" the poor, in the sense that the latter were to participate in the planning, administration, and distribution of the services. Pursuit of these two ends necessarily meant allocation of some CAP funds for community organization, particularly hiring and deploying in each neighborhood with a center men and women capable of recruiting and training indigenous persons with leadership qualities.

Some of CAA's staff workers stayed well within the ground rules laid down by City Council. Others were less circumspect, more or less frankly encouraging their "constituents" to articulate their covert grievances and to push their way into the political process, e.g. attend Council meetings *en bloc,* demonstrate before key city agencies, etc. Indeed, in a manner reminiscent of the massive unionization effort in the

middle 1930's, some CAA organizers came close to saying
openly that the statutory proviso of "maximum feasible par-
icipation" of the poor meant that "the President wants you
to organize for political action."

The CAA's official posture throughout the slow build-up
of its community-organization effort was one of denying the
effort's potential impact. Simple logic suggests, and the available evidence strongly supports, that the Agency not only understood where its policy in the centers might lead, but
hoped for that result. To put it plainly, without saying so,
the CAP's managers were by the end of 1967 abetting a policy of organizing the black poor into the city's political process and of building up a political base for the CAA as the
city's "chosen instrument" for the war on poverty.

By the end of 1967 limited progress toward attainment of
each of these goals had been registered. In advance of passage of the Green amendment to the Economic Opportunity Act, requiring that at least one-third of the membership
of community action commissions be representative of poverty-area residents, the Baltimore City Council had seen fit to
do just that. Moreover, collective pressure was generated on
behalf of the black poor in favor of direct election of "their"
representatives on the CAC. In tacit collaboration with
CORE, SNCC, and U-JOIN, among others, CAA's community organizers induced sizable numbers of inner-city residents
to make themselves heard at City Council meetings and confrontations with officials in the city's welfare, health, and education departments. Finally, in the mayoralty election of
November 1967 the large black population was for the first
time openly courted by the top of the Democratic ticket,
which won by a whopping 80 per cent of those voting.

CAA's drive to transform its impoverished "clients" into a
source of Agency power made less headway. Because so many
counter-forces were at work, it is hard to say which, if any,
was most responsible for the drive's painfully slow progress.

High among the contributing factors was the federally sponsored Model Cities program. Declared by the Administration and the Congress to be the chief means for welding an integrated effort on both physical and human renewal in the nation's urban centers, Model Cities was an obvious competitor with CAA for available money and manpower—the more so, because in its human-resources component Model Cities was required by law to incorporate all the features of the CAP: filling gaps in the array of services, co-ordination of service delivery systems, community organization, citizen participation, and so on. Though CAA was quick to see the threat posed by Model Cities and labored mightily to gain at least partial control over it, the Agency simply lacked enough muscle, i.e. its allies were too few and its enemies in high places too many. Far from commanding even a piece of the action, CAA was all but excluded from the processes of planning and later execution of the Model Cities effort.

At the close of 1967, then, the future of the CAA was very much in doubt, threatened both by loss of federal funds and by ill-concealed hostility on the local government's part. This was the price it paid for promoting political action among the poverty population and, in particular, in providing the poor an arena for conflict and a means of access to the political process. The price was high—but so may have been the value received.

BLACK ACHIEVEMENT OF POLITICAL ACCESS, 1968

By all odds Baltimore's most dramatic political event in 1968 was the several days of rioting in the inner city shortly after the assassination of Dr. Martin Luther King on April 4. Several features of the incident are noteworthy. In the first place, during 1964–67 when one major city after another experienced violent, large-scale riots by blacks, Baltimore had been riot-free. Various explanations, alone or in combina-

tion, were offered by whites and blacks alike for the city's
good fortune: skillful diplomacy on the part of the then-
Mayor, Theodore McKeldin; sensitive control of the police
by the state-appointed police chief; "responsible leadership"
by the main spokesmen of the black population; and probably most important of all, black passivity born for the most
part of resignation and apathy, but also of their abiding
faith that racial integration could be achieved through
peaceful means.

By 1967 there was surrounding white Baltimoreans an
aura of smugness and self-congratulation over the city's enduring freedom from mass violence. Even those who expressed fear for the future—"it's only a matter of time before
we're hit, too"—sounded unconvincing. Amongst the blacks,
however, we detected at the time a change in tone from that
sounded a year earlier. Their voices had become more stri-
dent, more self-assertive. Previously covert grievances were
stated openly. "Moderate" became something of a pejorative
label, like "Uncle Tom." Every act of white officialdom, governmental and private, was examined in terms of its impact
upon the relative position of blacks, and then almost invariably pronounced to be of a "racist" character. More often
accurately than not, blacks acidly described the city's highway
and slum-clearance projects as "Negro removal"; interpreted
all proposals for city-suburban co-operation as part of a con-
spiracy of whites to create a metropolitan government before
blacks could capture control of Baltimore's legislative and
executive offices; and bitterly assailed as discriminatory or
worse the policies and practices of the city's Civil Service
Commission, Department of Health, Department of Education, and Department of Welfare.

Undoubtedly, the new mood of exasperation and impati-
ence amongst blacks was partially a direct result of the "educational" work of community organizers. We suspect, as well,
that many blacks in the city more or less independently con-

cluded from their reading of events in other cities that black citizens could improve their relative position only through their own affirmative action. Reasonableness coupled with patience would achieve little or nothing, whereas it was the squeaky axle that got the grease.

The growing black intransigence was not significantly allayed by the new Mayor's prompt appointment of several blacks to key positions in the city government, positions heretofore always filled by prominent whites. The predominant view among politically alert blacks was that the Mayor had picked "safe" persons, whose appointment to sensitive slots would "cool out" the militants and their growing corps of followers. Even less charitably, the Mayor's appointments were derided by black militants as tokenism, pure and simple.

Black disenchantment with the Mayor was fed further by the latter's insistence from the outset that his chief function was to be honest broker among the competing interests in the city. This stance clearly implied that the blacks (and every other group), rather than forcing their way into relevant decision-making arenas and fighting their own battles, would have to deal through the Mayor, that is, count upon him to bargain on their behalf with all others and to deliver to them as much as he could get. The black leaders could not accept this mode of operation because it would have denied them the free and full access to the political system for which they had labored so long. Beyond that, they had no reason to believe, before the fact or after, that the Mayor could really deliver on any promises he might make to blacks.

Though no one knows for sure, it is most likely that young people made up the bulk of those who actually participated in the riots of April 1968.[2] Some of them were undoubtedly

2. Jane Motz, *Baltimore Civil Disorders, April 1968,* American Friends Service Committee (Baltimore, 1968), p. 18.

hoodlums, vandals, thrill-seekers. Few Baltimoreans will deny, however, that at base the riots were a symbolic expression of the pent-up frustration and anger of *all* blacks in the city's dark ghetto, even those who deplored the violence and property destruction. Put succinctly, "the disorders express[ed] black rage against white power." [3]

The riots had an even larger significance. For one thing, they were a new source of power for black leaders, who could now threaten to incite violence in the streets as the price of noncompliance with their demands. White and black leaders both recognized this: for example, in May 1968 the chief spokesman of the Interdenominational Ministers' Alliance, a longtime advocate of peaceful progress toward racial integration, declared publicly that unless a substantial number of blacks were hired by the City within a specified period of time, his group would stretch a chain across one of the city's busiest intersections and physically defend against its removal. The City acceded promptly to the demand.

This illustration points up another consequence of the April riots. Where previously, moderate black leaders sought their objectives within established political channels and in accordance with accepted values and procedures, many of them now were prepared, if necessary, to operate *outside* established channels and in defiance of accepted rules.

More than anything else, however, the riots apparently signalled the beginning of the end of the existing biased political system in Baltimore. No longer could blacks be excluded from it, denied access to the key centers of decision-making, prevented from gaining a greater share in the authoritative allocation of values. In the wake of the riots, long-standing covert grievances became overt and erupted into political conflict in a number of arenas. The Greater Baltimore Committee, once seen by militant blacks as an ally, now came under open attack over the issue of control of a federally

3. Ibid. p. 28.

financed model urban neighborhood project. In the face of opposition from prominent businessmen and a powerful arm of the governmental bureaucracy, black militants forced the Mayor to make a major concession in respect to control of the local Model Cities program. A proposed demonstration school with a racially balanced student body was angrily rejected by blacks, on the ground that they had not been fully involved in the prior planning of the project. There was a bitter public dispute over appointment of a new director of the Community Action Agency, the City Council finally refusing to designate the militants' nominee. Convinced that a judicial-reform proposal, which called for gubernatorial appointment with legislative assent rather than popular election of judges, would perpetuate white domination of the court system, black leaders waged an open campaign in opposition to it.

In prosecuting their position on each of these issues, the black militants in Baltimore demonstrated convincingly that they, as well as the whites, know how to exploit their political assets. A few details will drive this point home.

In mid-1968 the executive director of the Community Action Agency resigned his post after a three-year tenure, making no effort to conceal his belief that the Mayor and City Council were deliberately undermining the Agency in reprisal for its increasingly aggressive organizational activities among the poverty-area residents. The director's reading of the situation is supported by the available evidence. As was pointed out earlier, by the end of 1967 the CAA, with its black director in the forefront, was operating at full tilt and practically in the open to organize the black poor for political action. Among other things, CAA organizers helped "deliver" 800 persons to a Poor People's rally in the city; organized a protest demonstration at City Hall in support of a self-help housing proposal; allocated funds away from certain CAP components, such as day care and library services, in favor of efforts to organize tenant councils in public-housing projects and to stimulate groups of the poor to agitate for changes in educational and public-welfare policies and practices; and tried to block the establishment of "mayor's stations" throughout the city, on the ground that the latter were competitive with CAA's neighborhood centers. These activities understandably generated hostile reactions throughout the municipal government—department heads, the Mayor and the City Council. The Council's response, with the apparent agreement of the Mayor, was to refuse to appropriate funds that could be used by CAA for its organizational drive.

At this juncture the black members of the Community Action Commission tried to widen the scope of the conflict and, in the process, to invoke on their own behalf certain democratic values. Specifically, in a public statement protesting Council's refusal to appropriate funds, they declared:

> At last, we were to be given our well-earned right to work within the framework of a policy-making body, rather than vainly protest from without. Or so we naïvely believed.

> Instead, we have been forced to witness a steady reduction in the effectiveness of the program . . . we see no will, no commitment which can allow for the dynamic type of citizen participation which will break the endless cycle of poverty.

All the while the conflict over the CAP and its management was going on, a similar one was brewing over the Model Cities project, which could bring the city as much as $80 million in federal funds. Citing a guideline of the sponsoring federal agency, which called for maximum feasible participation of poverty-area residents, black leaders insisted that six newly incorporated Community Councils in the Model Cities area should be funded directly from Washington and given control over expenditure policy. This stance was, of course, in direct opposition to the Mayor's.

Faced with crises within both the CAA and the Model Cities planning group, and faced also with in-fighting between the two bodies, the Mayor moved to solve all three problems with a single stroke. The executive directorship of CAA was offered to the then-Director of Community Organization for Model Cities, himself a black activist. The offer carried with it the understnding that the new CAA director would have authority to co-ordinate the CAA and Model Cities neighborhood councils, an arrangement agreed to by both the U.S. Office of Economic Opportunity and the U.S. Department of Housing and Urban Development. City Council, however, refused to ratify the appointment, thereby provoking immediate reaction in the black population. A protest meeting was organized and blacks, moderates, and militants alike, resigned in a body from Baltimore's Urban Coalition.

In due course, the Mayor nominated and Council approved a new CAA director, a black man who was unlikely to be politically venturesome. As for control of Model Cities, the issue was at the end of 1968 still in limbo.

7

The Political Process in Baltimore:
Retrospect and Prospect

THE CHANGING IDEOLOGY OF RACE AND POVERTY

Until the late 1950's, Baltimore was a Southern city, in the important sense that a large white majority not only controlled the political machinery but systematically reinforced an ideology of white supremacy. One crucial consequence of this situation was that the grievances of Negroes, poor and non-poor alike, were almost totally prevented from becoming overt issues for decision. The problem of poverty was an overt issue, but only to the extent that governmental and voluntary agencies in the city carried on comparatively modest programs of general and categorical assistance to the impoverished. Aid to the poverty-stricken was rationalized mainly by reference to such traditional notions as *noblesse oblige* and the importance to the individual of doing good works for the less fortunate. Neither of these notions, it may be noted, contradicted the predominant ideology of divinely ordained white hegemony.

Now, a decade or so later, the ideological climate has changed markedly. Only a minority—and a dwindling one to boot—openly professes the dominant beliefs of yesteryear. Backed by injections of federal money, both governmental and private institutions in the city are carrying on programs to refurbish commercial and residential buildings, expand total employment, overcome the education and health problems of the poor, and promote greater political participation by all citizens, black as well as white. The situation in Baltimore, in short, seems to be moving toward what Jeanne Lowe detects in a number of other large cities: "There are remarkable new community coalitions; it seems a new era of localism has begun. Old ideological conflicts about public versus private, Republican versus Democrat, and federal intervention versus local autonomy have been buried locally for the cause of bettering our cities [among other things]." [1]

Although a clear majority accepts a credo of "fair shares" for all, politically and economically, its separate components hold differing views as to the exact meaning of fair shares and as to the speed and manner with which the goal is to be achieved. Some white "liberals," for example, accept, in principle, that the poor should have a voice in community decision-making. At the same time, these whites are fearful that greater participation of the poor, most of whom "don't know what they are talking about," will in short order convert the city into a Black Metropolis, with the whites cast in the role of oppressed minority. The white liberals' support of black militants is, therefore, distinctly restrained. The same may be said, although for partially different reasons, about certain elected officials. On one hand, they are keenly aware that the ideological framework has changed and that, in any case, blacks will soon be the city's majority group. On the other hand, they think it neither necessary nor advisable to break all their links with the persons and groups who want to keep the *status quo ante* basically intact, even if not completely the same. In a similar way, there are many advocates

1. Jeanne R. Lowe, *Cities in a Race with Time* (New York, 1967), pp. 556–57.

of equality in housing accommodations who would take a different view if they really believed that large numbers of the black poor would move into high-priced homes.

The evidence, in short, suggests that the majority in Baltimore is firmly committed, *in the abstract,* to an organized effort at reducing poverty among the blacks in the city. In practice, however, the zeal of most change-seekers in the white community is strongly tempered. One manifestation of this attitude is that they are content to let the federal government take the initiative in suggesting new approaches to the war on poverty. As a close corollary, local appropriations for anti-poverty programs are for the most part a reaction to federal grants-in-aid. In other words, it is the federal, rather than the municipal, government that is the main determining factor in the size and make-up of the governmentally sponsored anti-poverty effort in Baltimore.

NONDECISIONS AND NONDECISION-MAKING

If our definition of a key issue—any challenge to the power or authority of those who regularly enjoy a dominant position in the determination of policy outputs in the political system—is to be adhered to, it cannot be said that the controversies centering on race relations constitute key issues in Baltimore at the present time. As just noted, the predominant set of values has shifted in favor of equality of opportunity, and it is now hostile to the still formidable, but no longer dominant, lower-middle-class electorate and its leaders.

What *does* appear to be a key issue is the future distribution of power, authority, and influence between the white business, government, and political leaders, and the proletarian-based black groups and their leaders, who have been pressing directly and indirectly for a permanent and greater share in the decision-making process within the community.

Both sides are well aware of the existence of this underlying key issue. It is manifested in numerous concrete issues that involve the City Council, GBC, CAC, CAA, and other agencies and boards.

It is our conjecture that influential business leaders in Baltimore are utilizing the newly developed equal-opportunity mobilization of bias, not primarily to keep the "rednecks" in their place, but rather as a nondecision-making means of softening the militancy of leaders of the black poor and of gaining support among middle-class blacks, thereby diverting public attention from the question of what *actual share* militant organizations should have in the making of community decisions. According to this conjecture, both black militants and business leaders have used the issue of equal opportunity as a *means* to achieve different objectives: the black leaders to build a community power-base—which is a requisite to gaining greater decision-making power—and the business leaders to divert a threatening issue from the channel of policy choices.

A more direct means of nondecision-making open to the white establishment *vis-à-vis* the black population is co-optation of the latter's militant leaders. Because the militants are few in number, they are highly exposed to the blandishments of whites with something to offer—elective or appointive office, membership on governmental boards and commissions, employment in professional and administrative capacities. Some have found it impossible, in these circumstances, to remain true to "The Movement." Others have not only avoided co-optation, but have exploited their new positions for exerting leverage in a continuing struggle to build a power base in the inner city. These men seem acutely aware that a militant stance *vis-à-vis* the Establishment is essential to maintenance of their authority and influence amongst the black poor. Furthermore, their currently preferred position in the political process depends upon their continued militancy: stripped of it, they would be neither deferred to by the white leadership nor regarded as symbolically useful in supporting the legitimacy of the existing political system.

The black activist who accepts a place in the system puts himself, nevertheless, in an awkward position. He must steer a middle course. If he advocates or engages in violence, he will alienate the whites and if he too ardently supports the system, his black constituents will accuse him of selling out. U-JOIN's leader faced and neatly resolved this dilemma during the April 1968 riots. He mixed with the rioters and was actually arrested, but in no way did he implicate himself as either an instigator or practitioner of violent behavior.

White status-quo defenders have a problem, too, one that is largely of their own making. Fearful of erosion of their power, authority, and influence in the city, they have made numerous concessions to black militants while all but ignoring black moderates. In doing so, the whites have unwittingly nurtured their most aggressive challengers, lending credence to the latter's ideology and stimulating further demands for change in the existing still-biased system.

DECISIONS AND DECISION-MAKING

So far as anti-poverty and race-relations issues in Baltimore are concerned, there are no longer any insuperable barriers to entry into the decision-making arena. If there are covert grievances, they are so well concealed that we cannot locate them. With the possible exception of the key issue of the blacks' share in policy-making in the community, the channel of policy choices seems wide open.

It appears, therefore, that battles for change on poverty and race-relations issues will hence forth be won or lost in Baltimore's decision-making arenas: in the City Council which must enact the ordinances and appropriate funds, in the municipal departments and agencies which must administer the programs, in the state and federal agencies which establish the terms upon which grants-in-aid are given, and in the private institutions that provide employment, housing, and welfare services. However, although we lack enough evidence to generalize confidently, our strong impression is that the blacks' newly won access will not immediately produce sweeping changes in the size or character of anti-poverty and race-relations policy. This is not to say that the leaders (both genuine and self-styled) of the black population, and of the poverty population more generally, cannot and will not make any important gains in the months and years just ahead. As was pointed out earlier, they have already won some important battles. But much remains to be done. Baltimore still lacks an open-occupancy ordinance, still discriminates in the employment, retention, and promotion of blacks in both governmental and private institutions, still pursues a policy of frugality in its support of programs for the poverty population. Part of this pattern can be explained by reference to the diehard opponents of change. Some, perhaps more, of it can be laid at the door of those who see the need for change but want it to proceed at a more sedate pace and under their own leadership.

FEEDBACK

Even at this early stage in the process of change we can detect trends that portend a major reallocation of values in Baltimore. For one thing, the once-inert mass of blacks in the city is stirring perceptibly. An ever-greater number is becoming involved in the political process. How much of this activity is a direct outgrowth of the anti-poverty effort is immeasurable, but the programs have played a part.

What seems to be *the* major contributing factor to the process of political change has been the establishment in the city of federally financed programs designed to eliminate poverty. Without the federal grants-in-aid for its programs, Baltimore's anti-poverty effort would hardly deserve the name. Much more importantly in the present context, the anti-poverty agencies—CAA, Model Cities, and Model Urban Neighborhood Demonstration (MUND), among others— have been political catalysts in the city, chiefly because they have provided the black poor with a necessary means to organize for political action and to gain access to key decision-making centers. Specifically, they have made available to the poor:

(a) *Arenas of conflict.* The Community Action Commission, the Steering Committee of Model Cities, the Neighborhood Councils of MUND, and lesser arenas that have been established have given the spokesmen of the poor places to air their grievances and, more importantly, to engage the Mayor, the City Council, the public bureaucracy, and business interests in political combat on a key issue: control of anti-poverty policies and programs. The fight for control of Model Cities, reported above, is a good case in point.

(b) *Sources of power.* These sources include political and legal knowledge, organizational skills and facilities and leadership. The CAA, for example, has established 44 neighborhood centers throughout the inner city that provide meeting places, advice, and encouragement to neighborhood groups and individuals. In being alert to translate grievances into power issues, CAA's community organizers have given people the initial impetus for joining or creating a protest organization and the self-confidence and guidance to effectively engage in political action.

(c) *Incentive for conflict.* Projects such as Model Cities and MUND, which call for expenditure of millions of dollars and which will affect tens of thousands of people, cannot but invite controversy as to what group or agency should control them. Because representatives of the poor now possess the means for creating such a controversy and, because the question of control over public projects remains unsettled, it is reasonable to assume that the poor will press their demands for a share of control. Indeed, as we have seen, they have already done so.

(d) *A doctrine of legitimacy.* What critics, such as Daniel Patrick Moynihan, overlook is that "maximum feasible participation" is a doctrine which has served to legitimatize the demands of the poor for a significant share in the decision-making process.[2] Despite its ambiguity, which has provoked continuous conflict, it has afforded a forceful ideological justification to the poor and their leaders for taking control of the funds and the policy-making of the various local projects. The appeal of what might be called the ideology of participation has by no means been confined to leaders of the black poor. A growing number of the poor themselves are aware of its existence and believe strongly in it. These feelings were manifest, for example, in the refusal of a group of low-income parents in Baltimore to allow their children to engage in an enriched, integrated school experiment because those who had proposed the experiment had excluded the low-income parents from participating in planning it.

To restate, federal programs and federal funds have been the main means, directly and indirectly, by which the black power have gained a foothold in Baltimore's political system. The programs and money have helped directly by enforcing the administrative guidelines on citizen participation in planning and distributing services. They have helped indirectly in that the poor are increasingly being enlisted to support different local welfare agencies in their competition for a larger share of the city's available funds. And, to return to the proposition made at the start of this sub-section, federal grants for programs have helped to raise the expectations of a large and growing percentage of the poverty population,

2. Daniel P. Moynihan, *Maximum Feasible Misunderstanding* (New York, 1969).

thereby causing them to develop a set of interests and to make use of the political system in furthering their interests.

How firm is the black poor's political foothold? Have they now won or will they soon acquire sufficient power, authority, and influence to gain permanent access to the political process in Baltimore and to improve significantly their share in the over-all distribution of benefits and privileges? The verdict is not yet in. The struggle continues.

On the affirmative side of the question, we can repeat that the effort by and on behalf of the poor to acquire political leverage is no longer covert and nearly stifled, but rather is taking place within newly created arenas of conflict and decision-making. Furthermore, the federal government, which was chiefly responsible for creating the opportunity for the poor to organize politically, has not yet ceased to sustain the effort by and for them. To be sure, the great majority of the black poor in Baltimore remains unorganized and virtually powerless. They are, however, becoming ever-more politically aware, are prepared to employ newly established channels of communication and decision-making arenas to assert their rights and press home their demands, and have already compelled their white antagonists to give some ground. Still further, black leaders in the city now exercise a modicum of authority, that is, a small, slowly growing number of whites in key decision-making centers accede to black demands because they share the blacks' values.

There are also counter-forces at work. Initially, white racism is far from dead in Baltimore. As we said earlier, only a minority of white Baltimoreans still adamantly oppose equality of opportunity, let alone equality of outcomes for blacks. These "open" racists consist for the most part of the so-called rednecks, persons in the lower-middle-income brackets who are fiercely defensive of their hard-won socioeconomic gains in recent years and who resent having to contribute to the uplifting of the "undeserving" people on lower rungs of the ladder.

To the unabashed racists there must be added a much larger (but still uncounted) number of "covert" racists, i.e. persons whose attitudes, often not conscious, cause them "to respond to a situation in a different manner when blacks are involved than when whites only are involved." [3] A very substantial proportion of white property owners falls into this category, including not only certain inner-city landlords, but affluent individuals in the "outer city" who admit they would move to the suburbs in preference to having black neighbors. Many, probably most, Baltimoreans who grumble noisily about high local taxes too readily throw the blame on welfare recipients, who "everybody knows" are black and undeserving, not to say chiselers on the public purse. Covert racism persists among employers, governmental and non-profit as well as private, and certain trade unions. And fifteen years after *Brown v. Board of Education,* covert racism in various forms lingers in the public schools and colleges in Baltimore. Because blacks gained their current foothold in the face of endemic racism, it is tempting to infer that the rest of the ride is downhill. That may prove to be the case, particularly if the disparate racist sub-groups find no reason or are unable to coalesce in opposition to black power. On this score, no prediction seems safe.

A second negative factor from the point of view of Baltimore's blacks is their own internal divisions. As expected, we found that the local branches of the NAACP and the Urban League have a different view of the world than do CORE, SNCC, and U-JOIN. To be politically effective, these and other black groups must make common cause, but thus far they have done so only infrequently and for but brief periods. Moreover, if and as more blacks in the city are "co-opted by the system," in the sense that they move a rung or two up the socio-economic ladder, The Movement may be seriously weakened. This is simply to say that as the black

3. Roscoe C. Brown, "The White University Must Respond to Black Student Needs," *Negro Digest,* XVIII (March 1969), pp. 30–31.

bourgeoisie slowly grows in number, two things may happen: the gainers will become more benevolent toward the established order and defensive of it; while those left behind will interpret their own failure to advance as stemming purely from personal inadequacy and will give up the fight.

A third counter-pressure against growing black power may prove to be the most telling of all. As was argued previously, federal anti-poverty programs backed with federal funds and federal endorsement of the principles of maximum feasible participation have played a central role in the black drive for political access. Emasculation of the federal effort before the blacks' political foothold can be expanded and consolidated could be devastating. There are ominous signs that that very thing may be in process. Not only are Congressional appropriations for CAP's, Model Cities projects, and the like being cut below their comparatively modest levels of earlier years (on the debatable grounds that national security and control of inflation have higher priority), but also opponents of citizen participation are becoming increasingly emboldened. Daniel Moynihan's recent attack on maximum feasible participation is little more than an elaboration of the status-quo defenders' theme that government has no call to subsidize "local revolution." Equally, much of the enthusiasm for sharing of federal revenues with state and local governments, in lieu of programmatic grants-in-aid, stems from those eager to strengthen the less-restrictive but still existing mobilization of bias. The same applies to the mounting pressure in Congress to promote regional and metropolitan interjurisdictional cooperation.[4]

4. Arnold Schuchter is one who sees this point: "This planning concept [he writes] undoubtedly will be unacceptable to many Negroes who are beginning to see the concept [sic] of power fulfilled in city politics." He goes on to argue, however, that "the politics of the dispossessed are [sic], in the long run, working against the economic and social viability of urban life in major cities—for blacks or whites." (Arnold Schuchter, *White Power/Black Freedom*, Boston, 1968, p. 374.)

CONCLUSION

We have attempted in the last three chapters to analyze how power, authority, and influence were brought to bear in two contrasting periods in shaping and sustaining political beliefs, institutions, and procedures which, in turn, affect the distribution of outcomes among persons and groups in Baltimore. In the first period, it appeared that power was primarily exercised in the form of nondecisions that contributed to the maintenance of a system that prevented certain groups in the community from being heard. The distribution of outcomes among groups during this period was not substantially altered. In the second period, ideological and institutional changes of considerable magnitude were brought about through key decisions that were initiated and shaped by the exercise of power on the part of those who had been previously excluded from the political system. These decisions both reflected and contributed to a change in the distribution of outcomes in the community.

Baltimore has, in effect, gone far toward satisfying the Kerner Commission's recommendation that an opportunity be provided "for meaningful involvement of ghetto residents in shaping policies and programs which affect the community." This outcome stemmed not from a voluntary decision by the white majority in the city, but from a show of power by the black poor's leaders. Armed with power resources supplied by the federal government, the black leaders significantly altered the political process. Further changes along these lines are likely, but when they will occur, what form they will take, and how they will be effected is, of course, a matter of conjecture.

8

Toward a General Theory of the Political Process

As students of the political process, our ultimate objective is to develop a general theory, that is, a set of interrelated hypotheses which can be repeatedly confirmed by different empirical analysts. We are frank to admit that we have not yet attained this goal. It is our hope, however, that the theory presented in this essay significantly advances the state of the art of political analysis. To clarify our position and thereby facilitate others' appraisal of it, we conclude by summarizing our main propositions:

   1. As Harold Lasswell put it many years ago, politics has to do with who gets what, when, and how. Till recently, however, political analysts, theoretical and empirical, have lavished attention upon "who" and "how" to the virtual exclusion of "what." It is the latter, relabeled "policy output," which is our initial and principal focus. We are, of course, concerned with who seeks to exercise power over whom and in what ways, but we are no less concerned with the allocation of values (including power) at a point in time and over

time. Put yet another way, we focus both on who gets what and how, and who gets left out and how.

2. Polities are rarely, if ever, characterized by equality in the allocation of values. Almost invariably, the policy outputs of the system benefit some persons and groups more than others. Moreover, inequality in the distribution of benefits and privileges tends to persist through time.

3. Political systems tend consistently to develop a mobilization of bias, a set of values, beliefs, rituals, and procedures which can be exploited by beneficiaries of the unequal value-allocation to defend and promote their preferred position.

4. Polities will be found in which there is consensus on the prevailing distribution of benefits and privileges, i.e. in which there are no change-seekers, overt or covert. This kind of situation is atypical. In most polities the investigator will discover actual or potential challengers to the prevailing order.

5. The dominant group or groups in a polity exercise power and its correlates to maintain and strengthen the existing mobilization of bias. Although challenges to its or their preferred position can and will be fought within the channel of policy choices, those in a position of dominance lay particularly heavy stress upon preventing the disaffected from raising issues that are threatening to the former's preferred position.

6. Subordinate groups, because of their insufficient power resources in relationship to the restrictive political system, are often unable to convert their demands for change into important political issues. As their grievances grow and as they come to conclude that non-violent protest will be to no avail, such groups not uncommonly back their demands by the threat of violence or by actual violence. (The threat of violence is a source of present power; actual violence is a means of acquiring future power. Resort to violence, and even the threat to do so, can also have the reverse effect, by

decreasing—even shattering—the resources of power, authority and influence of those who invoke violent action. See pp.
29–30 above.)

7. More or less permanent shifts in the mobilization of
bias, and the value-allocation that flows from it, are brought
about primarily because the previously disfavored persons
and groups have gained additional resources of power and
authority, usually from movements or institutions outside
the polity in question.

The reader is cautioned that, although these seven propositions lie at the core of our argument in the previous chapters, they constitute bare bones, not the fullest and most rig-
orous statement of our position. We must also stress that
each of the points is a tentative generalization, subject to empirical verification, not a purported statement of fact.

We began this essay by criticizing both the "sociological"
and "political-science" approaches to study of community
power, on the ground chiefly that both lead to foreordained
conclusions. We are deeply persuaded that our approach
avoids this pitfall. To repeat ourselves, we ask neither "Who
runs things here?" nor "Does anyone run things here?" but
rather "Is the distribution of benefits and privileges highly
unequal and, if so, why?" Within this framework of reference the empirical investigator is in a position to discover
not only the current state of affairs in the polity, but also to
observe in a period of transition the manifold utilization of
power and its correlates in relationship to ideology, institutions, and the political behavior of actors within and outside
the system.

Appendixes

APPENDIX A

The Politics of Local Government in Baltimore

RONNIE GOLDBERG

This report is the result of a study of Baltimore's City Council. As such, it is neither a complete nor definitive report but, rather, an introduction composed of details garnered from two months of not-always-incisive research. If parts of the information to follow appear irrelevant, it may be because the author hesitated to make too many deletions from a necessarily limited store of information. By the same token, the absence of information that may seem to informed Baltimoreans to be obvious and/or vital must be attributed to the limited duration of the research.

I

The Baltimore City Council forms the legislative branch in a Mayor-Council form of government. It is currently composed of eighteen Councilmen, three elected from each of the city's six Councilmanic Districts,[1] and a Council Presi-

1. Councilmanic districts were reapportioned in 1966. Before this, there were 20 members, three of each of the four districts with fewer than 70,000 reg-

dent, elected at large. All have four-year terms. The Council
President is next in line of succession to the Mayor, assuming all official duties in case of the latter's illness or absence.
The President, of course, presides over the Council and may
vote on all issues before it. He is also the President of the
Board of Estimates (to be discussed below). Should the
Council President be judged guilty of a misdemeanor, in-
competence, or willful neglect, he is subject to preferment of
charges by the Mayor and removal from office by a two-
thirds vote of the Council. If for this reason (or any other
one) the President should fail to continue in office, a temporary successor is elected by the Council from outside its own
ranks. The Council also elects a Vice-President by majority
vote from among its own members. The Vice-President receives a higher salary than the rank and file of the Council,[2]
and is empowered to assume the President's duties in his absence.

The Council itself is organized into twenty-one committees. The most important [3] are the Committees on Zoning,
Building Regulations, Public Transportation, Budget and
Finance, Executive Appointments, and the Judiciary
Committee.[4] Each committee has seven members (with the
exception of Zoning, with eleven), named by the Council
President and approved by a majority of the Council. Here
we find one great area for factional disputes, a subject to be
discussed later.

istered voters and four from each of the two districts with more than that
voter population. For further details on the 1966 reapportionment, see "The
Politics of Reapportionment in Baltimore," Appendix B.
2. The 1964 Council salaries (since raised) were as follows: Council member,
$6,500; Vice-President, $7,250; President, $15,000.
3. Their degree of importance is directly related to matters of patronage and
political leverage, and will be discussed in a subsequent section of this report.
4. Other Committees are Aviation, Claims and Disbursements, Education,
Harbor, Health, Highways and Franchises, Housing, Intergovernmental Relations, Labor, Parks and Recreation, Ways and Means, Traffic, Rules, Public
Utilities, and Public Relations.

The Council as a governmental body is responsible for all legislative acts. These are entered in Council in the form of either proposed ordinances or resolutions. Upon introduction, unless otherwise ordered by unanimous consent or a two-thirds vote, a prospective ordinance is read by title and assigned by the President to the appropriate Council committee. The committee holds public hearings on the bill and ultimately reports to the Council, either favorably, unfavorably, or without recommendations. If the committee does not act upon a bill within six months (notification is given it one week before the end of the six-month period), the bill is withdrawn. However, a majority of the Council may require a committee to return a proposed resolution to the floor. In this case, the proposal comes as if reported "without recommendations." A majority of the Council may also fix a day by which pending resolutions must be reported out.

Councilmanic rules require that before passage, a bill must be read in Council on three separate occasions. The committee report thus marks the second reading. (Bills returning to the floor after recommittal are also considered to be at the second-reading stage.) The third reading of an ordinance becomes its final trial. Should it be passed by simple majority vote, it is sent to the Mayor for final approval. Bills not acted upon by the Mayor within five Council sessions automatically become law. The Mayor's veto may be overridden by a three-fourths majority. A bill may be killed at any reading, but after defeat may be returned to committee and reintroduced. Another means of "saving" a bill is a motion for "reconsideration," which may be made if the original motion is still in the possession of the Council.[5] A motion to reconsider is passed by a majority of those present, but the motion itself must be made by a Councilman wishing to change his vote. Amendments to bills may be accepted as

5. Council is considered to retain possession of a motion for up to three meetings after the most recent vote was taken.

late as the third reading, in which case the bill is reprinted before final passage.

Among other things, the City Charter empowers Council to investigate any municipal agency, and gives authorization for its committees to administer oaths and summon witnesses. Council is also empowered to remove the City Comptroller by majority vote and elect a temporary replacement, and to remove its own members at will by a three-quarters majority vote. Expulsions must be made on the grounds of disorderly behavior or misconduct, and are subject to review by the Baltimore City Court. Council may also adopt its own rules of procedure, which require a two-thirds vote to be suspended.

Finally, Council must approve all executive nominations for appointment. This provision explains the importance of its Executive Appointments Committee, to which all nominations are referred (these must be reported out by the next meeting, unless otherwise specified by majority vote, and are considered approved if not acted upon within three meetings). The proviso also indicates one area in which Council may gain some degree of leverage over the Mayor—particularly when the Mayor's political-party affiliation differs from that of a Council majority, as was the case from 1963 to 1967.

One potential source of mayoral power, authority, and influence does exist, however, in the Board of Estimates, a city department which, on the basis of estimates submitted by city agencies, determines how available public revenues are to be allocated among the Mayor's Office, Council, and municipal departments and agencies. As was previously mentioned, the Council President is the Chairman of the Board. The other members are the Comptroller, the Mayor, and two appointees of the Mayor. Although the Mayor can, in principle, command a majority of the Board, he is not free from Council influence. Not only must his Board appointments be consented to by Council, but Council may vote to decrease (but not increase) the budgetary allocations of the Board. Council thus has an indirect veto over proposed new programs, notably including those to which the city government must contribute if federal funds are to be secured.

II

We now turn to the character of each of the six Councilmanic Districts and their representatives in Council.[6]

The First District, with the Sixth, is predominantly a white working-class area with racist and conservative overtones. Before the 1966 redistricting, Negroes made up 8.4 per cent of the First's registered voters; they now account for about 11 per cent of the total. The black population has been, and still is, politically impotent. All three of the First District's present Councilmen were incumbents re-elected in November 1967 without serious challenge from any organized Negro groups. All three have also been consistent in their votes against all kinds of civil-rights and anti-poverty legislation.

Redistricting has affected the Second District more profoundly than any other. Prior to 1966, the Second was extremely small and, therefore, over-represented. Forty-nine per cent of its registered voters were Negro, most of them poor, inarticulate, unorganized, and therefore politically impotent. As a result of redistricting, the Second gained a middle-class group of Negroes at the expense of the Third, where they had been too much in the minority to be of much political influence. The Second District also lost to the First a number of poorer Negroes. Now, 54 per cent of the

6. The entire Council is Democratic. See discussion of two-party system in Section III.

Second District's registered voters are Negro, who have be-come the object of concerted efforts, notably by CORE and U-VOTE,[7] to increase their political participation. The im-mediate result of these efforts and the redistricting has been the election of a Negro Councilman from the Second. The District's two other representatives, however, appeal strictly to its "poor-white" elements, who seem mainly interested in preventing full racial integration and in delaying full Negro political participation as long as possible. We may note in passing that the Second is the site of the city's strongest Re-publican organization, one that is largely black.

Negro voter registration in the Third District was de-creased from 18 per cent of total registrants to 3 per cent as a result of redistricting, making the Third the "whitest" of the Councilmanic Districts. Although it includes upper middle-income residents, large segments of the population are lower middle-income whites with a "conservative" political orien-tation. However, in the November 1967 Council election, the spokesman for this lower middle-income group was de-feated by a young "liberal" lawyer. The other two Third-District Councilmen may be described as "middle of the roaders," leaning uncertainly toward the "conservative" side.

The Fourth District is the locus of most of the Negro vot-ing power there is in Baltimore. An overwhelming 79 per cent of the District's registered voters are Negro, who in 1963 elected the city's first two black Councilmen. Since the Nov-ember 1967 election, the District has been represented by three of the Council's four Negroes. When we turn to the discussion of factional politics (Section III), we will see that the once-potent white-dominated political "machines" in the Fourth District have all but lost their influence. Now politi-

7. The Baltimore chapter of CORE belongs to the national organization. Its resources are limited; financial difficulties almost closed the office at one point in 1967. It is still functioning, however. U-VOTE was a grassroots organiza-tion formed for the specific purpose of voter registration.

cal influence in the District is largely divided between two rival Negro factions.[8]

The Fifth District is essentially a "middle-class" area. About 29 per cent of its registered voters are Negro. In addition, the District has a large Jewish population, especially in its northwestern sections. It is in the northwest that the old-time political bosses [9] retain their power. As the Fourth District became increasingly Negro, the Jewish community, a large part of which included small businessmen, moved westward to the Fifth. Many of these persons have grown wealthier and, in the process, have tended to become politically more liberal. Interestingly, voters in the Fifth have elected two Councilmen who can be counted upon to support civil-rights legislation and the CAP, and a third Councilman who has been a consistent enemy of Baltimore's anti-poverty program as well as a foe of open occupancy in housing, Rent-Defense, and comparable legislation. Strongly linked to the aforementioned political machine and liked and respected by his constituents, the third man retains his Council seat in spite, rather than because of his views.

In the Sixth District Negroes now number 40 per cent of all registered voters. Before reapportionment in 1966 the proportion was only 29 per cent. As sizable as this increase was, however, it still was not large enough to elect a Negro representative in Council. In fact, only one Negro candidate appeared on the Democratic primary ballot. Negroes in the Sixth are fairly well concentrated in one area, while the rest of the District is composed of a large "redneck" element. The politics in the Sixth closely resemble those in the First District; all three Councilmen have lower middle-income or-

8. One of these, which has been called the "Black Bourgeoisie," has elected two candidates to Council. The other, closely associated with the NAACP, has the Director of the Baltimore City Community Action Agency among its members.
9. Notably Jack Pollack. See Section III.

igins and attitudes. It seems likely that Negroes in the Sixth
will be denied Council representation until they gain a nu-
merical edge on the whites.

III

The last time the two-party system functioned in Baltimore
was 1927, when Council was composed of nine members
from each party. Now the city is solidly Democratic. The
notable exception to complete one-party rule came most recently in 1963, when Republican Theodore R. McKeldin
was elected Mayor. His election, however, was generally interpreted as more a demonstration of his personal popularity
and prestige than of any resurgence of the Republican organization. Since December 1967, the city once again has a
Democratic Mayor and a totally Democratic Council.

One of the most important results of the lack of vigorous
party rivalry is sharp division within the Democratic Party
itself; inter-party competition has been replaced by intra-
party, factional struggle. Two factions in particular have
dominated Council politics. Of the two, the one run by Jack
Pollack has been the most tightly organized. Candidates have
come to Pollack because he could provide the men and
machinery necessary to engineer a victory, chiefly by concentrating his manpower on "his man" at the expense of any
other. The candidate, in return, pledged allegiance to Pollack, helping the latter reap the patronage that kept the political machine going. What is more important, an economic
base was formed behind Pollack, as vested interests, particularly property owners, could get his assurance that certain
bills would or would not be passed. It is important to note,
in this connection, that the Pollack faction has had neither a
liberal nor a conservative ideology. Indeed, on issues which
have had little bearing on the present and future health of

his political organization, Pollack has been studiously neutral.

The strength of his organization reached its peak in the early 1950's, but now is on the wane. The growth of Negro population and political power in his former domain, the Fourth District, and the development of a liberal Jewish population in the Fifth have combined to reduce sharply the number of votes he can deliver to a given candidate. Consequently, Pollack must form alliances with others, in order to get what he wants from Council. These coalitions, it should be noted, tend to be fragile, shifting from time to time, and even from issue to issue.

The second main Democratic faction consists largely of those not associated with the Pollack organization who must, in self-defense, vote together. This faction is headed by Mayor (formerly Council President) Thomas D'Alesandro. Held together in part by the strength of the D'Alesandro name at election time, the bloc is a loose coalition, which in the past has derived most of its strength from the First and Second Districts.[10]

In circumstances where all or nearly all Councilmen are aligned with one faction or another, intra-party strife can reduce the Council to legislative impotence. In the middle 1960's, for instance, control of the key positions in the body hung in the balance for a period of months, during which time the legislative process was virtually paralyzed. Moreover, in an environment where the overriding consideration in all questions is patronage, the true issues behind Council proposals often get lost in the shuffle. It is not unusual for a Councilman to vote with his faction in a way contrary to the vital interests (or expressed desires) of his constituents. Nor

10. Intra-district political factions are also important. Within each District various Democratic clubs put up candidates for the Democratic primary, where a victory is synonymous with election.

is it unusual for the discussion in Council to be irrelevant to
the issues involved.

IV

We have seen that the Mayor has virtually no formal control
over the City Council. Consequently, he must rely on indirect means of asserting his will, the most obvious of which is
(again) patronage. Mayor McKeldin's situation was notably
poor in this regard. He has been accused of being unwilling
to use his patronage powers, for example, to trade for passage of a bill barring racial discrimination in use of public
accommodations. It is difficult for an outsider to judge the
validity of this accusation, but we must recognize that as the
City's only elected Republican, the Mayor's political leverage must inevitably have been small.

Now, however, the Mayor is not only a Democrat, but one
who has been President of City Council and whose running
mate in 1967 is the current President. The opportunities for
Mayor-Council co-operation will no doubt abound in the
coming session. To some extent Mayor D'Alesandro's success
will depend on the extent to which he can unite the warring
factions in the Democratic Party. It will also depend, perhaps more so in the future than now, on his success in win-
ning the not overly enthusiastic Negro community. Certainly
his 78 per cent majority portends well.

It is still too early to assess the new Mayor and Council,
but one or two final observations seem to be in order. First,
Negro representation in City Council is not as large as was
hoped or as would be warranted by the racial composition of
the city. Furthermore, on the surface it would seem that the
"conservatives" still have a grip on the Council. There does
seem to be some change in its traditionally "working-class"
orientation, however. The election of young professionals
from the Second and Third Districts may be indicative of

some new trend. The first true tests of the Council will only be seen in the votes yet to come.

Finally, we must not forget the extent to which the anti-poverty effort is dependent on the Council. Immediately upon approving the Community Action Program, the Council made the CAA a city agency, thereby gaining financial control over all anti-poverty programs. The Council thereby not only asserted the right to "investigate" the CAA but, by withholding the city's contribution, to virtually veto any new program-proposal.[11] We can therefore scarcely overestimate the importance of the Council to anti-poverty activity in Baltimore.

11. City governments *must* contribute or the Federal government will withhold funds.

APPENDIX B

The Politics of Reapportionment in Baltimore

BRENDA L. DAVIES

I. INTRODUCTION

The political component of our evaluation of the anti-poverty effort in Baltimore City has two central concerns. First, what are the forces, personal and impersonal, that shape and implement anti-poverty policy in Baltimore? Second, what directions will anti-poverty policy probably take in the future, assuming that (a) the determinants of the political process remain substantially the same, and (b) the determinants, and therefore the process too, undergo significant change?

Preparatory to empirical research, we developed an analytical framework, which is embodied in the text above, Chapter 4. Summarized briefly, we postulated that in any polity there are, on one hand, persons and groups who want to bring about change in the existing allocation of those values that affect a significant number of persons in the community and, on the other, persons and groups who wish to keep things as they are. Both "change-seekers" and "status-quo defenders" have resources which permit them to exercise power, authority, or influence in order to attain their ends.

The change-seekers typically start, however, from a comparative disadvantage: there is a "mobilization of bias" in the polity, a set of beliefs, myths, institutions, and procedures which deters change and therefore buttresses the position of those opposed to change. The latter, moreover, tend systematically to reinforce the mobilization of bias.

In order for change to take place, those seeking it must break through a series of barriers. First, they must get their demand into the "channel of policy choices." Next, they must gain access to the decision-making arena. Third, they must command a voting majority among the decision-makers. Finally, they must assure that the decision is effectively implemented.

To test these and related notions, we decided to examine a number of issues which had actually arisen in Baltimore in the recent past. One product of these inquiries would be a better understanding of the process by which grievances enter the channel of policy choices and, one way or another, are resolved. Beyond that, we anticipated that the issue-studies would afford insights as to the mobilization of bias, i.e. the nature of the barriers to change, the manner in which they are utilized to block or dilute demands for change, and the identity of those who benefit from preservation of the status-quo.

The specific issue with which this paper is concerned is a community-wide conflict during 1966 over Baltimore City's Councilmanic voting districts. As most, perhaps all, of those involved recognized at the time, the way in which the issue was resolved affected not only the short-term make-up of the City Council, but also and much more importantly, the future "output" of the political system with respect to anti-poverty policy, race-relations policy, and the distribution of deference and welfare values in the city.

II. BACKGROUND TO CONFLICT

Dimensions of the Problem
Division of Baltimore City's voting population into six districts dates from 1923, when a Charter revision transformed the City Council from bicameral to unicameral form. At that time, the Council consisted of 18 members, three from each district, plus a president elected at large. This scheme endured until 1946, when the Charter was amended to authorize, among other things, a fourth Councilman in any district with more than 75,000 voters. Because two of the six districts satisfied this criterion, Council membership increased thereafter to a total of 20, plus the president.

As is true of most political jurisdictions, Baltimore's post-1947 districts were of very different sizes. This is well depicted in Table I, which reports voting population by district and by race in 1966:

Table I. Voter Registration by District and by Race.
Baltimore City, 1966

DISTRICT	TOTAL VOTERS	WHITE VOTERS		NEGRO VOTERS	
		TOTAL	%	TOTAL	%
1	37,790	34,617	92.0	3,173	8.0
2	30,068	15,383	51.0	14,685	49.0
3	131,135	107,526	82.0	23,609	18.0
4	48,055	13,865	29.0	34,190	71.0
5	114,673	63,030	55.0	51,643	45.0
6	47,274	33,665	71.0	13,609	29.0
TOTAL	408,995	268,086	65.5	140,909	34.5

Although the Third and Fifth Districts had four Councilmen, as against the others' three, voters in the Third and Fifth were still grossly underrepresented. To cite the most outstanding comparison, each Councilman in the Third District represented a *population* of nearly 69,000 and a *voter registration* of roughly 33,000, whereas each Second District

Councilman represented a *population* of about 28,000 and a *voter registration* of only 10,000. A vote in the Second District, therefore, was worth 3.3 times as much as a vote in the Third. As can be seen in Table I, black voters constituted a majority in only one of the six districts. They made up a 49 per cent minority in the over-represented Second, a 45 per cent minority in the under-represented Fifth. What is more important, although Negroes made up over 40 per cent of the city's population and more than a third of its registered voters in 1966, only one member of the Council—just 5 per cent of its membership—was a black man.

The Issue Becomes Overt

It is moot how long this situation would have been endured without change, had the U.S. Supreme Court not ruled in 1962 (*Baker v. Carr*) that the Constitution of the United States required apportionment of legislatures on the one-man, one-vote principle. The Court's decree had, at least, a galvanizing effect. On one hand, under the prodding of a Circuit Court judge, the General Assembly of Maryland undertook to revamp Baltimore City's legislative districts, assigning the task in late 1962 to a House Committee composed exclusively of Delegates from the city. Of more importance for present purposes, in April 1963 a Negro prominent in Baltimore City politics sued for court reapportionment of Councilmanic districts, contending that as a voter in the Fifth District, he was grossly under-represented in the Council and that because the existing membership was elected from malapportioned districts, it could not and would not redraw the lines properly. Plaintiff further prayed that the 1963 elections to City Council be deferred until redistricting had been accomplished.

The city government's response was prompt. The day before the suit came to court, the Mayor announced the appointment of a seven-member commission, charged with drafting more equitable district-boundary lines. Heading the commission was Dr. Harry Bard, a well-known local educator with strong ties to affluent and traditionally "liberal" white groups in the city. A variety of other "interests" was represented on the commission, notably including the City Council itself.

The Bard commission began work in April 1963, seeking to devise a scheme which would be suitable for both legislative and Councilmanic districts. This task, it must be observed, was of heroic proportions, because the City Charter called for districts based on voter registration, while the Maryland Constitution prescribed legislative districts based on total population. Nonetheless, in a matter of days after its organization the commission produced what proved to be only the first of its plans, this one dubbed Plan X.

Prompt support for Plan X was given by the Mayor and the City Council President, each urging its adoption before the local election in May 1963. Their haste was understandable: of the 20 members of Council, eight were not seeking re-election, therefore had no vested political interests which would prevent them from voting for Plan X. Opponents of the latter were able, however, to defer action on it until after the election. Thereupon, the Council itself drew up and voted approval of an alternative scheme.

The Council's proposal, which was called Modified Plan X, was in many respects the mirror image of the conflicting factions and interests that make up the law-making body. The overwhelming majority of voters in Baltimore are registered Democrats. The Republican party is little more than a hollow shell. In 1963, as a result, every major elective office in the city was held by a Democrat. Whatever political competition there was stemmed from intra-, not inter-party, rivalries—rivalries manifested in shifting coalitions based much less on ideological differences than upon the distribution of deference values (power, authority, and influence) and welfare values (wealth, income, etc.).

Modified Plan X was slated for voter action in the general election of November 1964, some 18 months in the future. In the interim, however, the State legislature under threat of court action undertook anew to devise a scheme for reapportionment of legislative districts in Baltimore City. Helped in their effort by Dr. Bard, the General Assembly in March 1964 adopted a plan strikingly similar to Councilmanic Plan X.

How did Plan X and its legislative-district equivalent compare with the Council-approved Modified Plan X? Interestingly, neither provided for districts of equal size: probably in order to win the support of voters in the Third and Fifth Districts, both proposals left the two oversized districts intact and awarded them four Councilmen, as against the three assigned to other districts. Similarly, the Assembly-approved plan provided that each district have two Senators, but a varying number of Delegates. The chief aim of all planners, in short, was to reduce inequity in the number of residents or voters per Councilman or Delegate, not in the size of the districts.

The central difference between the competing schemes was that Plan X and its Assembly-approved counterpart were more equitable than the Council-backed proposal. This difference is well illustrated by the way each dealt with the First District. Under Plan X the First District would have 16,667 voters per Councilman, or 12.5 per cent less than the city-wide average of 19,100. Under Modified Plan X, by contrast, the First District would have only 13,900 voters per Councilman, 27 per cent under the city-wide average.

The plans differed in one other important respect. Although none significantly rearranged the distribution of Negroes by voting district, Modified Plan X provided for the transfer of some predominantly white precincts from the

Fifth District into the heavily Negro Fourth. This adjustment was apparently made at the behest of an influential
political leader, who had dominated Fourth District politics
until his white constituency there had moved into Fifth District wards.

Scheduled for a referendum vote in November 1964, Modified Plan X was stricken from the ballot a month before
the election. Ruling on the suit originally brought before
them in April 1963, three Federal judges declared that Modified Plan X violated the equal-protection clause of the Four-
teenth Amendment to the Constitution of the United States,
in that it was not based on population. This meant, in effect,
that because the City Charter provided otherwise, the
Charter would have to be amended. The court also ruled
that the plan would result in discrimination against voters
(many of them Negroes) residing in the proposed Second
and Fourth Districts. They observed, specifically, that under
Modified Plan X one more Councilman would be assigned
to the Fifth than to the Fourth District, notwithstanding that
the Fifth had roughly 4,000 fewer residents than the Fourth.
Furthermore, the plan also resulted in a weighting of voters
between the First and Second Districts, so that a vote in the
First would be worth 1.66 times a vote in the Second.

In its decision, the Court recommended that City Council
adopt a plan that would be ready for voters' approval by
November 1966. The Court observed pointedly that it would
retain jurisdiction of the case.

The Bard Plan

A new commission on redistricting was created by the Mayor
in January 1965. Again headed by Dr. Bard, the commission
consisted of 18 members and consultants—five political-science professors, four members of City Council, and nine persons representing such organizations as the Junior Chamber
of Commerce, AFL-CIO, Women's Civic League, League of

Women Voters, the major political parties, and well-established political clubs. Though the commission's membership was predominantly white, the city's black population was represented. The commission laid down four guidelines for itself: (a) "The districts should be based on the judicial 'one man, one vote' pronouncements. Deviation from the average in population should be as near o per cent as practicable; (b) Districts should be composed of contiguous territory and be as compact as possible; (c) Due regard should be paid to the integrity of neighborhoods and the natural dividing lines of the City's various sections; (d) Favorable consideration should be given to the existing ward and precinct lines, the newly created legislative districts, and the probabilities of acceptance by the City Council, the electorate and the courts." [1] None of these objectives, it will be seen, was stated in truly operational terms, which made their attainment more difficult than otherwise. Of more importance, the objectives were in partial conflict with one another, a point exemplified by the fact that certain Councilmen on the commission insisted successfully that the boundaries to be proposed for their individual districts be drawn to their own specifications.[2] Still further, the fourth guideline both promised and proved to be unusually hard to abide by. The existing districts were, as has been said, grossly out of line with the requirements laid down by the federal court. Substantial changes were called for, changes which would almost certainly threaten the political position of one Councilman or more.

The commission presented its reapportionment plan to City Council in mid-May 1965. It recommended the follow-

1. Minutes of Mayor's Commission on Redistricting, February 26, 1965, p. 1.
2. Dr. Bard's original draft provided for the election of some Councilmen on an at-large basis. At least one Councilmanic member objected to this notion, on the ground that to win election to an at-large seat, a candidate would have to strike costly bargains with each of six district "bosses." By a close vote, the at-large proposal was defeated within the commission.

ing changes in the existing districts, each of them to have
three Councilmen:

a. The First District would gain seven precincts from the
Second District. In three of the seven there was a predominance of impoverished Negroes, the other four contained an
admixture of lower-middle-income and low-income whites,
Lumbee Indians, and Negroes. The First District would also
gain ten precincts, almost exclusively white in racial make-
up, from the Third District. From the Fourth District, the
First would gain one precinct, virtually all residents of
which were black. Finally, two wards with a black:white population ratio of 2:1 would be added to the First District at
the expense of the Sixth. The upshot would be that the First
would be enlarged by 56,000 persons, of whom 19,000 were
registered voters. The District would also become more diverse in racial composition than it had been. Significantly,
however, almost two-thirds of the added voters would be
white persons, most of whom had been politically inactive.
In these circumstances, it is no wonder that First District
political leaders, whose position depended at the time upon
a voting majority of "working-class" whites, put up only
slight resistance to the Bard commission's proposals.[3] On the
other hand, there were muffled outcries from the Negroes
who would be transferred from the Fourth District to the
First. As things stood, these persons lived in a predominantly
(79 per cent) black area, were represented in City Council
by a Negro, and had limited access to City patronage. The
Bard plan would deprive them of these advantages by moving them into a district dominated by whites with a history
of antipathy to the city's black population.

b. The Second District, which was the smallest of the six,
would become the largest. Most of what it would gain would

3. Their only serious complaint had to do with assignment to the First District of the two Sixth-District wards with their total population of 6300 low-
income persons, white and black.

come from the Third, although three precincts were also taken from the Fourth. The upshot of the proposed changes would be to make the Second more diverse with respect to income classes, but virtually the same in racial composition (48 per cent Negro, rather than the existing 49 per cent). Specifically, the eastern end of the district would encompass the east side of Baltimore's "inner city." In the south-eastern corner would lie "Bohemia," the lower-middle-income area populated mainly by persons of Czechoslovak descent. The western end of the district would consist of whites in differing income strata. All reports indicate that more than the usual amount of bargaining among politicians, both Negro and white, underlay the commission's proposals for the Second District.

c. The Third District, one of the two largest as things stood, would be diminished substantially in size, losing nearly 100,000 inhabitants. In terms of registered voters, it would lose over 8000, virtually all of them white, to the First District, and roughly 34,000, half of them white, to the Second District. The proportion of Negroes in the Third District, after reapportionment, would be less than 8 per cent, as against 18 per cent under the existing arrangement. Also, the District's representatives in City Council would fall from 4 to 3.

d. The Fourth District was already heavily Negro in character. Under the Bard commission's plan, it would gain over 32,000 persons, of whom nearly 29,000 were black, from the Fifth District and would lose three predominantly white precincts to the Second District. The Fourth, in short, would move even closer to a uni-racial makeup, its voter registration rising from 71 per cent Negro to 79 per cent.

e. The Fifth District, like the Third, would also shrink in numbers and Council representation. As just mentioned, it would lose over 32,000 persons, mostly Negro, to the Fourth District. In addition, it would surrender several precincts, most of them with a high percentage of black persons, to the Sixth. As a result, the black:white ratio in the Fifth would fall sharply from the 45:55 ratio under the existing scheme.

f. Although the Sixth District would give up two wards, both predominantly Negro, to the First District, it would gain several heavily Negro precincts from the Fifth. The total size of the Sixth District would therefore increase. The racial composition would remain about the same, the losses of black residents approximately offsetting the gains.

Despite the Bard commission's effort to arrive at a politically feasible scheme, its proposal promptly came under sharp attack from three different sources. The Councilmen from the Third and Fifth Districts, each of which were currently alloted four seats in the legislative body, objected because two would necessarily lose their seats. The Council delegation from the First District opposed the addition to their constituency of the predominantly Negro wards detached from the Sixth District. Councilmen and political leaders in the Fifth District, anxious to regain their control of the Fourth District, were unhappy because the commission failed to add a significant number of white voters to the latter area.

During the summer of 1965 the Bard Plan, as it came to be known, languished in Council committee. In September of that year, a Councilman from the Fourth District, himself a Negro, offered a substitute ordinance that provided for 20 districts, each with one Councilman. This proposal attracted enthusiastic support in some quarters, particularly Republicans and civil-rights groups, chiefly because it promised to bring about greater Republican and Negro representation in City Council.[4]

Faced with the court-imposed constraint that an acceptable plan be put before the voters in November 1966, the

4. At the time, Negroes constituted 40 per cent and Republicans 16 per cent of all voters—with some overlap between the two.

Council majority continued to search for options. By early 1966 a new possibility was under consideration, namely, adopting the Bard-Plan districts but providing for six additional Councilmen-at-large. Designed to win over those Councilmen in the Third and Fifth Districts whose seats would be eliminated under the Bard commission's proposal, the at-large amendment was opposed mainly on the ground that the expense of an at-large campaign was so great that candidates would be "owned" by the political organizations in the city. Beyond that, the fear was expressed in some quarters that certain district organizations would coalesce in favor of certain at-large candidates to the detriment of others.

In May 1966, still another reapportionment plan was brought forward, this one under the sponsorship of one of the two factions that dominated Democratic politics in Baltimore. Introduced by Councilman Arthur Best and depicted as adhering more closely than the Bard Plan to the one-man, one-vote principle, the plan provided for the transfer of precincts among districts such that only one would have a Negro majority. The exception was the Fourth District, where the plan would reduce the proportion of Negroes from over 70 per cent to only 54 per cent. Population differentials among the districts would be smaller than under the Bard Plan, but two of the other four guidelines for reapportionment (see above, p. 127) were all but disregarded: (a) the Best Plan districts corresponded not at all with the legislative districts, and (b) the boundaries were drawn in such a way as to impair seriously the "integrity" of the existing districts. In short, the Best Plan had all the earmarks of a blatant exercise in gerrymandering.

In early June of 1966 the City Solicitor opined publicly that the Best Plan was unconstitutional. Thereupon, yet another proposal was put before Council under the sponsorship, of its President (now Mayor), Thomas D'Alesandro

III. The new scheme provided simply that there be six districts of equal size, each with four representatives in Council. This proposal, together with the Best Plan, came before the lawmakers in late June. On the first test, neither scheme won a majority. On the second division, however, the Best Plan was approved, 11 to 9.[5]

III. RESOLUTION OF THE CONFLICT

Widening of the Scope

With the Court-imposed deadline for a general referendum on reapportionment less than five months away, those Councilmen whose oxen were gored by the Best Plan broadened the scope of the struggle. In particular, they appealed to interests in the community that heretofore had not become directly involved in the struggle.

Three days after the Council's vote in favor of the Best Plan, Councilman Parks convened a public meeting of about

---

5. The voting pattern, shown below, is suggestive of the lack of organizational discipline within the districts or, to put it another way, the extent to which individual Councilmen had to choose among conflicting political loyalties. As can be seen, excepting only the First, there was no district whose representatives voted *en bloc,* one way or the other.

FOR		AGAINST	
Panuska	(2nd)	D'Alesandro	(President)
Best	(3rd)	Bonnett	(1st)
Gallagher	(3rd)	Duffy	(1st)
Pica	(3rd)	Staszak	(1st)
Dixon	(4th)	Ward	(2nd)
Soypher	(4th)	Curran	(3rd)
Caplan	(5th)	Parks	(4th)
Edelman	(5th)	Schaefer	(5th)
Rubenstein	(5th)	Hines	(6th)
Myers	(6th)		
Leone	(6th)		

Councilman Prucha (2nd) abstained, possibly because he concluded that neither plan was congenial to his political future.

twenty civic and civil-rights leaders in a Masonic temple. Nominally chaired by an active proponent of the Negro cause who was also Grand Master of the temple, the gathering included representatives of two civil-rights organizations, recently formed and (by local standards) highly militant: the Union for Jobs or Income Now (U-JOIN) and the Congress of Racial Equality (CORE) Target City Project. Unalterably opposed to the Best Plan, these two groups strongly backed the Bard scheme, subject to the proviso that it be modified so that the Second District, like the Fourth, would have a Negro voting majority. In this demand, they were supported by an aggressive white politician from the Third District, whose main interest was to have an upper-income white area, assigned by the Bard commission to the Second District, incorporated into the Third.

This minority coalition proposed to the assemblage a series of modifications to the Bard Plan, as follows:

  a. Move a predominantly Negro ward from the First District to the Sixth, and at the same time move a largely white ward from the Sixth District to the First.
  b. Move a large number of whites from the Second District to the First.
  c. Move a sizable number of Negroes from the Third District to the Second, offsetting this by moving a cluster of upper-income whites from the Second District to the Third.

Were these changes to be adopted, the Second District would indeed have a Negro majority (54 per cent); the white population of the Third District would be enriched, numerically and economically; and the white majority in the First District (all of the Councilmen from which had opposed the Best Plan) would be substantially increased.

This package of proposals was put to a vote. With only mild dissent from a minority of four, the package was approved. Of more than passing interest, Dr. Bard himself was

present at the meeting but offered no objection to any of the
proposed amendments to his plan.

Defining the Issue

With this important preliminary out of the way, the proponents of what soon came to be known as the Modified Bard
Plan girded themselves for an effort to get their scheme on
the referendum ballot. Toward this end, they created a committee of four—one representative each from the League of
Women Voters, the Junior Chamber of Commerce, the
Urban Commission of the Catholic Archdiocese of Baltimore, and the Federation of Civil-Rights Organizations—to
map a petition drive.

As all the participants perceived, the way in which the
issue was defined would bear heavily on its final resolution.
Specifically, if the ad-hoc group promoted the Modified Bard
Plan on the ground that it would reduce political inequity
between whites and blacks, it might well be defeated by the
"backlash vote." Indeed, as soon as the group announced its
version of the Bard Plan, opponents to it charged that the
proposal was the handiwork, not of a bi-racial coalition but
of the black-dominated Federation of Civil-Rights Organizations. Proponents of the Modified Bard Plan had to stand on
higher ground, namely, electoral equality for *all* citizens,
white as well as black. As a tactical corollary, the drive to get
the plan on the ballot and approved by the voters had to be
led by prestigious whites, with the Negro leaders and organizations keeping well away from center stage.

Accordingly, the ad-hoc group organized a blue-ribbon petition committee, consisting of a majority of prominent
white persons; several of whom had served on the Bard commission. Only three of the 13 members were Negro, all of
them with respected positions in the community—a college
president, a social scientist, a key administrator in the Urban
League—and none identified closely with any militant civil-

rights organization. Significantly, however, the persons who actually circulated the petitions were mainly Negro civil-rights workers. The latter and their allies [6] performed a minor miracle: in a period of three weeks they obtained 21,000 validated signatures, more than double the minimum number required to have the Modified Bard Plan put on the ballot. What's more, roughly 8000 of the signatures were gotten in mid-summer in East Baltimore, the heart of the city's poverty area.

This activity did not go unnoticed. Councilman Ward of the Second District, who had supported the ill-fated D'Alesandro Plan against the Best Plan but strongly opposed the Modified Bard Plan, launched a counter-drive to get the *original* Bard Plan on the ballot. In part because of poor organization, the effort failed: only 7000 names were obtained on the Ward group's petitions, 3000 less than the required minimum.

By the end of July 1966, therefore, the lines were sharply drawn. On one side were the supporters of the Modified Bard Plan, promptly renamed (for an obvious reason) the Fair Bard Plan. Opposing them were the proponents of the equally (but accidentally) well-named Best Plan.

The Decision-Making Process
Throughout August, September, and October 1966 the Fair-Bard backers mounted a remarkable voter-education campaign throughout the city. Initially, public endorsement of the plan was obtained from a variety of the city's most prestigious civic, religious, educational, and philanthropic leaders and associations. What was far more important, a massive ef-

6. The League of Women Voters was made responsible for gathering signatures in the middle- and high-income white areas of the city. Woman Power, Inc., an organization of Negro business and professional women with ties to the Democratic political organization in the Fourth District, circulated petitions in West Baltimore. Republican leaders and workers, CORE and U-VOTE (an offshoot of U-JOIN) were assigned the East Baltimore area.

fort was undertaken, especially in the poverty areas, to regis-
ter new voters and to instruct all voters on how to cast a ballot; voting in this particular referendum was especially difficult: in order for a vote to truly count, the elector had to
vote "No" on one plan *and* "Yes" on another.

The Fair-Bard proponents had other problems to contend
with. For one thing, they had to forestall an attempt, perhaps abetted by the opposition, to place the reapportionment questions at the bottom of the election ballot, where
they might well have "gotten lost." For another, barely a
week before the election the Fair-Bard group discovered that
(a) the Best Plan was listed on the ballot above the Fair-
Bard Plan, (b) the Best Plan was clearly identified on the
ballot as concerned with Councilmanic redistricting, while
Fair-Bard was simply labeled a "Charter Amendment," and
(c) a darker shade of ink was used for the Best Plan than
that for its rival. By resort to pressure, persuasion, and a
measure of good luck, the Fair-Bard backers succeeded in obtaining a new set of ballots with which they had no serious
complaint.

On November 8, 1966, the issue was finally resolved. Question A, the Best Plan, was resoundingly rejected and Question B, the Fair-Bard Plan, almost as resoundingly approved.
Although the margin in *favor* of Question B was smaller
than that *against* Question A, the latter was rejected by a
majority in all voting districts, while the former was approved in all districts.

IV. SOME CONCLUDING REFLECTIONS

The working hypothesis which this case study was designed
to test may be restated simply. To bring about change in the
existing authoritative allocation of those values that affect a
significant number in any community is a very difficult task,
if the change-seekers are confronted with a determined

group of status-quo defenders. This is not to say that value-reallocation is impossible. It is to say that the odds in the conflict between proponents and opponents of change are typically very much in favor of the latter.

Superficially, the controversy over reapportionment of Councilmanic districts in Baltimore arose from and revolved entirely around the question of how to abide by the Constitutional requirement of one-man, one-vote. As the foregoing account makes clear, however, this was neither the only nor even the most important issue. Quite the contrary, the central question from beginning to end was whether Baltimore's black population was or was not to be represented in City Council in accordance with its size. The evidence to this effect is overwhelming.

First of all, it was a Negro citizen who made the issue overt by means of a suit brought under the authority of the U.S. Supreme Court's ruling in *Baker v. Carr* (1962). Second, although none of the many reapportionment plans that were proposed was attacked or defended by reference to the way it assigned Negroes by voting district, each plan was initially scrutinized and judged in these terms. Third, and as a close corollary, the chief difference between the two plans that appeared on the ballot was that one promised to enhance the political representation of black people, while the other promised to limit it. Fourth, although Negro-led groups had to and did play an indispensable role in the Fair-Bard drive, they willingly worked under semi-cover out of fear of a massive white "backlash." For the same reason, both blacks and whites in the Fair-Bard camp carefully depicted their proposal as assuring electoral justice to *all* voters, not merely to Negroes.

From the standpoint of those opposed to significant change in the size and composition of the districts, the racial aspect of the struggle was both beneficial and detrimental. On one hand, the status-quo defenders could count on the support of that sizable segment of the city's white population which was, in one degree or another, anti-Negro. The "racists" or "rednecks," in short, were an important source of power for the leading opponents of change. On the other hand, the demand for change came at a time when the segregationist ideology that had long predominated in Baltimore was fast giving way to one based on the concept of equality of opportunity. In other words, those who had lately been cast in the role of white knights were now seen by a majority as "heavies."

The status-quo defenders were unable either to prevent the reapportionment issue from entering the channel of policy choices or from reaching the decision-making arena. Their failure stemmed not from a lack of trying. The original Bard Plan was pigeonholed in favor of one much more to their own liking. A final vote in City Council on the Best Plan was delayed until less than five months before the referendum, and barely three weeks before the deadline for submitting petitions for a counter-proposal. When the Fair-Bard supporters began circulating petitions to get their scheme on the ballot, their opponents organized a counter-effort, striving in particular to get signatures of those who had already signed the Fair-Bard petition—thereby invalidating *both* signatures. To top things off, the Best Plan supporters attempted to "rig" the ballot in their own favor.

It is often the case that demands for change are gutted or killed at the implementation stage, therefore never become effective policies. That fate did not befall the Fair-Bard reapportionment scheme, which took full effect in the general election of November 1967. It is too early to say much about its feedback effects. Fragmentary evidence suggests, however, that the impact will be substantial. Heartened by their success, various Negro leaders and groups are pressing harder than ever for other changes that will benefit them and their "constituents." An indeterminate but sizable number of black citizens became involved in the political process for the first time; some of them have remained involved, in order to press their newly won advantage. And at a very specific level, the referendum victory appears to have been a factor in City Council's approval of a long-stalled self-help housing program for the poverty population and for its approval of a controversial system of rental allowances for public-welfare recipients occupying substandard housing.

Key Actors in Baltimore's Anti-Poverty Public

JAMES R. TAYLOR

The first body of results to be reported here consists of a description of the structure of the Baltimore system as it appeared to the investigators during their research. In large measure this section is thus intended to be factual and noninterpretive and to provide a base line for evaluating other parts of the report. Naturally, the description given here makes no pretense whatever to being comprehensive in the sense of taking in all the forces, actors, or structural elements which may go into the formulation of public policy in Baltimore. It is necessarily selective in that the attention is focused primarily on government departments and refers to other actors only to the extent that they appeared to the investigators to impinge rather directly on bureaucratic affairs. Even within the perspective of the operations of the government departments, this section is very much skewed toward matters which more or less directly concern the poverty program. This introduces a further distortion which should be borne in mind. It is to be hoped, nevertheless, the description contained here, however biased it may be by the considerations outlined here (and no doubt others), may yet provide a clear and useful background to the interpretation which follows later.

The charter of the city of Baltimore sets out the responsibilities of twenty departments. A certain number of these have rather specialized functions—the Board of Ethics, the Art Commission, the Departments of Assessments, Aviation, Fire, Transit and Traffic, Municipal and Zoning Appeals—and were arbitrarily excluded from the present study as having apparent minimal salience to questions related to antipoverty programs. Of the remaining departments, a logical classification might be as follows: (1) agencies of central control (Department of Finance, Department of the Treasurer, Department of Law, Department of Legislative Reference, Civil Service Commission); (2) agencies responsible for provision of physical services (Department of Public Works, Department of Recreation and Parks, BURHA;[1] (3) agencies responsible for provision of human services (Department of Health, Department of Welfare, Department of Hospitals, Department of Education, Department of Recreation and Parks); (4) central planning departments (Planning, BURHA, etc.). The departments of Recreation and Parks and BURHA have been included in two categories because of their mixed functions. Planning might also have been mentioned as an agency of central control, since its functions include to a considerable extent the reviewing of and passing on a number of programs evolved by other agencies. In any case the classification is arbitrary—it is intended simply to serve a useful purpose in relation to the presentation of findings.

The list given above is by no means comprehensive. The Police Department, for example, is formally run by the state but functions very much within the city structure. One of

1. Baltimore Urban Renewal and Housing Agency, since raised to departmental status.

the most important of departments (and one which is tied closely to the federal government through HUD) from the point of view of its relationship to the anti-poverty program is BURHA, which, while heavily committed to the provision of physical services, also maintains a community development service, and judging from interviews with its senior officers, feels a strong commitment to maintain a balance between the physical and human aspects of its work. Agencies such as the Bureau of Building Inspection and Sanitation were treated as independent, for the purposes of the present study, though they fell under the administrative jurisdiction of the Department of Public Works. Other agencies contacted during the course of the investigation include the Community Relations Commission and the Economic Development Commission. Finally, the Community Action Agency might be included to complete the list of those agencies which fell within the study. In addition, senior officers of the Maryland State Employment Service were interviewed since their functions lead them to be deeply involved in the anti-poverty effort.

Not all agencies received equal attention during the study. Criteria employed to decide on which agencies would be most carefully studied included the following three: (1) the size of the agency, (2) the salience of its functions to the anti-poverty effort, and (3) the desire to achieve a balanced picture in the sense of including adequate representation of the four major types of department. Throughout, the researchers received full co-operation from all officials contacted and had no difficulty in arranging interviews with them.

Of the agencies of central control, the Department of Finance and the Civil Service Commission appear to be the most important in relation to the anti-poverty program. A senior analyst in the Department is assigned nearly full-time to deal with the Community Action Agency, an indirect acknowledgment of the complexity of its diverse experimental programs. Adequate support from the Department of Finance is necessary to pass the hurdles of the Board of Estimates and City Council. As a general rule, departments submit their spending requirements to Finance, who prepare a general budget, with recommendations appended thereto. Since many of the CAA requests tend to be in the form of "crash" programs, they often make special demands on Finance.

The Civil Service Commission controls, or processes, almost all appointments to city government (the exceptions are in the Department of Public Works, which has a certain number of casual labor jobs which it handles without reference to the Commission). Civil Service Commissions historically were established to eliminate the abuses of the patronage system, and that also appears to have been the case in Baltimore. Appropriately, efforts were made to insulate it as far as possible from political pressure. Thus, the Mayor, in making his appointments to the three-man Commission, is instructed by the Charter that "All appointments to the Civil Service Commission shall be made from persons friendly to the 'merit system' of appointment to office." Since one of the expectations of the CAA is that it develop indigenous leadership among groups characterized often by their lack of formal qualifications for appointment and promotion in the public service, a degree of conflict of aims followed from the creation of the CAA, and indeed there is evidence of some inevitable tension between the two agencies.

One other central body, while small in size, is important. This is the City Council Office of Fiscal Review. The professional advice emanating from this office to the Board of Estimates and City Council obviously has weight in the decisions made by elected officials.

Among departments concerned with physical services, the largest and most important is the Department of Public

Works. It controls a large number of jobs, not all of which, as noted above, fall within the domain of the Civil Service Commission. More than any other department it is susceptible to pressures from the political domain to find work for constituents. Since it controls the city's Building Construction Bureau, the letting of numerous contracts is handled through this department. Through its sanitation and building inspection activities it is related in other ways to the problems of the slums. Particularly in the area of building inspection it finds itself at the center of conflicting pressures, from civil rights groups—and from the CAA—for increased code enforcement, and from landlords whose interest is not necessarily in stricter enforcement of the building code. Council itself reflects these conflicting pressures. The Director of Public Works is a member of the Board of Estimates and thus has a voice in fiscal decisions. Probably no other department has such complex interrelationships with the main set of actors in the political process.

BURHA is deeply committed to improving the physical environment of the city. Originally, this department was two departments, but the two components of Urban Renewal and Housing were united by the simple device of appointing the same individuals to their different boards and uniting them under a single director. The department is thus responsible both for public housing and for relocation, renewal, and rehabilitation services. In addition, the agency early developed a community relations service. Finally, its activities naturally link it with the Planning Commission in developing a long-term plan for the city. Thus, in the most real sense the activities of BURHA tend to overlap with the concerns of the CAA, though the main focus of concern differs in many ways.

All of the departments concerned with human services— Health, Welfare, Education, Recreation, Hospitals—overlap directly with the area of activities of the CAA. Health reports, for example, that 80 per cent of its activities are directed to the Action Area residents. Probably a not dissimilar percentage of Welfare services fall in the same area. Problems of slum youth occupy an increasing part of the attention of Education and Recreation. Again, these departments take on a number of the third-party contracts given out by the CAA. If we add the community services of BURHA and the activities of the Maryland State Employment Service, some idea of the degree to which CAA activities impinge on the existing bureaucratic structure may be gained. Problems of co-ordination of services existed before the creation of the CAA, but there seems no doubt that they have been intensified by pressures engendered by the new agency and by a growing awareness by all concerned of the social dynamite which exists in the slums.

THE DEPARTMENTAL STRUCTURE AND THE NATURE OF THE PROBLEM

Traditional line departments in Baltimore, as in other cities, were not designed with a problem such as poverty in view. Public works, Education, hospitals, Parks, even Public Welfare were meant to supply necessary services to a thriving, healthy community in those areas where private initiative was unable, or unwilling, to take on the job. They provided the necessary sub-structure underlying the range of other activities in which a basically middle-class community was engaged. Problems of co-ordination were minimal. In many cases, departmental autonomy was fostered deliberately. Thus, for example, early in this century the Department of Education was weaned away from direct political involvement in order to prevent abuses in the appointment of teachers. The creation of numerous boards and commissions occupied by prominent citizens placed barriers to the direct manipulation of departmental policy by political interests and, practically, reduced the power of the Mayor to involve himself directly in the work of the departments.

The problem of poverty, on the other hand, is that of a sick community. Its citizens are undereducated, live in over-crowded quarters which in turn engender sanitation and health problems, lack access to employment opportunities, are underserviced in such simple things as adequate street lights, police services, etc., are discriminated against in a multitude of ways of which discrimination on the basis of color is only one, and lack the diversity of organizations of one kind or another through which citizens of a community normally achieve their common goals. The composite of inter-related problems which characterize the over-all problem of urban poverty makes demands on city departments which none of them can resolve by themselves. Education founders because of the social and psychological problems of the students; social problems emerge from high unemployment and severely overcrowded living conditions; but unemployment has as one of its causes the lack of motivation and training of people living in the slums. In turn, a healthy community needs to be built on a sense of pride of ownership and accomplishment, but few slum businesses in fact foster indigenous pride when the prevailing conditions are so discouraging to entrepreneurship. The people of the slums feel themselves to be, and in large measure they are, excluded from a voice in the community's vital activities. The old-line departments appear impotent to deal with the problem in any satisfactory way.

In response to the pressures of urban physical and social decay, certain steps have been taken. Attempts, for example, have been made to introduce some measure of co-ordination of departmental activities. A so-called "Conservation Committee" has been established under the chairmanship of the Mayor's co-ordinator. For whatever reason, the Committee has not been very effective. The Mayor has also established a

series of "task forces" with wide community representation
to consider some of the major problems of the city and come
up with policy proposals. While these task forces have had
several useful effects, they have left the problems of a common attack on the massive problems of poverty largely un-
touched. A third type of approach—and certainly the most
ambitious—is best exemplified by the CAA itself. In this case
a new department of government has been established whose
direct responsibility is to attempt to deal with the problem
as a whole. The concept of a broad-front attack on a massive
problem through the agency of a single department did not
originate with the CAA, however. BURHA, which preceded
the CAA by some years, was similar in some respects in its
all-enveloping concern for the total environment. The evolu-
tion of BURHA in its present form may be significant: originally its aims were more limited and more directly patterned
after traditional line departments.[2] It may also be significant
that one of the early moving spirits in the "Plan for Action,"
which was the blueprint for the present CAA, had functioned as a Chairman of BURHA.

The investigators did not find unanimity in support of
setting up the CAP in Baltimore as a department of government, though the majority of individuals interviewed appeared to agree with this basic decision. The city originally
had the option of establishing a public or non-profit corporation outside the formal government apparatus, as has been
the course followed in a number of other cities with CAP
programs. The findings of this study indicate that Baltimore's decision was consistent with other elements in the city
life. Most of the individuals who supported the establishment of a CAP in Baltimore wanted a balance between ex-
perimentalism on the one hand and control over the program's activities on the other. In practice this decision ap-

2. The use of the term "line department" is intended here to refer to an
agency which is assigned well-delineated functional responsibilities.

pears to have had advantages and disadvantages. It has imposed constraints on the program (in hiring, to give only
one example); on the other hand, it has resulted in top
officials of the CAA in Baltimore being included directly in
important decision-making processes. The consequences of
this latter will be discussed further below.

The creation of an agency of government to deal with the
problem of poverty as a whole has pointed up the incapac-
ity of the traditional bureaucratic system to deal with the
multidimensional demands imposed on city government by
the existence of massive slum conditions; nevertheless the evidence does not indicate that setting up an agency such as
the CAA has resolved the problem, either. In some cases the
CAA's activities have overlapped with those of other departments, with the result that new problems of co-ordination
have been created. In other cases, the existence of the CAA
has resulted in intensified demands for services on the old-
line agencies, demands which they have been unable or unwilling to meet. The CAA lacks the fiscal or human resources to cope with even the problems in its target areas, let
alone the total problems of poverty in the city. It may be
argued, and our research indicates that many officials in the
city feel, that one of the principal benefits of the CAA's comparatively aggressive and experimental approaches has been
to demonstrate the inadequacies of the traditional departmental approaches. This point of view holds that the basic
problem of how to mobilize even the existing services within
the city, and what new initiatives remain to be built in, is
now the basic issue facing Baltimore. This point of view further contends that both the mechanisms of how to develop
dynamic policy at the supra-departmental level, and how to
incorporate departmental policy—at present piecemeal and
non-articulated—within any comprehensive framework and
coordinate diverse departmental activities, is the central
challenge facing the city. Even those who take the more lim-

ited view that the CAA is a less effective means of reducing poverty than simply giving the old-line departments more funds would be, also concede that they have learned from its existence, and that even the old-line agencies need to change.

THE DEPARTMENTS SITUATED IN THE
LARGER PICTURE OF BALTIMORE

It is somewhat easier to understand the full picture of government departmental structure and activities by situating them within the larger context of the Baltimore system as a whole. The activities of city departments often impinge directly on those of other actors within the overall system of the city, and vice versa. Often links with elements in the larger system—of ideology and interest—are closer than with other government departments. This is more likely to be the case where, as in Baltimore, departments enjoy no little measure of autonomy from direct political intrusion in their day-to-day activities. These links are, however, formal as well as informal. Thus, the titular heads of several agencies are not the full-time professional civil servants who direct their operations, but the chairmen of commissions or boards who are drawn from the ranks of interested citizens. This structural device helps to assure that departmental policy will be adjusted to the concerns of interested influential actors in the city at large. It is probably true in any case that, through informal mechanisms, senior departmental decision-makers would tend to make common cause with others outside the bureaucratic structure who were in a position to advise them or to support them in developing policies they considered desirable, but the participation of citizens, required by the city charter, in the numerous boards and commissions ensures a measure of interaction. The CAA is itself headed by a commission—the CAC—and the composition of that commission has been the center of some controversy, an indirect confir-

mation of the importance of the pattern of relationships existing between agencies of government and other actors in
the system.

THE MAYOR'S ROLE

The actors who are most directly relevant to the government
departments are, first, the Mayor, and second, City Council.
The Mayor, as head of the Administration, controls appointments of top departmental officials, decides who will sit on
commissions and advisory boards, may require any department to make an accounting to him of its spending, and has
the means in his power to influence the setting of departmental policy. In theory at least the Charter gives him all
the power necessary to set the tone and pace of the city's
business.

In fact, the situation is not quite so straightforward. Baltimore, like other cities, has had its share in the past of passive
Mayors who allowed departments comparatively free rein (if
inadequate funds) and did little to strengthen the Mayor's
office. The present (1967) office-holder is a Republican, facing
an all-Democrat Council. Informants described him unanimously as a sincere civil-rights advocate from far back in his
career. They agree that he has stood behind the CAA consistently and seen that its spokesmen had a voice in all matters
which concerned them. He has given them funds to the extent that it was in his power, and has done much to mobilize
community support in a number of ways behind their programs. On the other hand, except in crises, he has not attempted to provide strong leadership for the departments as
a whole in any concerted attack on poverty, more than the
moral leadership of his own example. Co-ordination has not
noticeably improved under his regime. An outgoing, gregari-
ous man, he has used his office to keep in touch with wide
segments of the community, and some observers credit his

going unhesitatingly to the places where people live to talk with them and to listen to their problems with keeping Baltimore free from the destructive riots which have afflicted similar cities. Whether or not that is true, it is certain that the time spent in contact with the public could not be spent in study of the administrative problems of the bureaucracy. The Mayor in Baltimore is further constrained by the absence of real staff support. The Mayor's staff is tiny, a handful of assistants only, and has no hope of keeping abreast of the considerable complexities of departmental activities, let alone being active in the developing of creative policies. It was reported to us that one of the legacies of the present Mayor who leaves office this fall will be a set of recommendations for improving the staff situation of the Mayor's office.

A Republican Mayor in Baltimore has a weak political organization behind him. The present incumbent appears to have filled this gap by establishing a number of contacts with certain active segments of the community. The Mayor, for example, has co-operated extensively with senior members of the business community, the investigators were told. He has been closely in touch with a number of the leaders of civil rights groups. One mechanism he has used extensively is what is termed in Baltimore "task forces." These are *ad hoc* committees with broad mandates from the Mayor to look into some of the city's problems and to come up with recommendations for policy. The task force on equal rights, for example, is divided into six committees: Education, Housing, Police-Community Relations, Public Accommodations, Employment, Health and Welfare. Each committee has two co-chairmen, one white, one Negro. They meet fairly regularly while the task force itself meets once a month. It appeared that a certain amount of useful work had been done by the task force approach, but without an effective staff organization to do the hard spade work of translating ideas into programs, the impact on the organizations of government seems

not to have been great. It should be noted, however, that the
subjects taken up by the task force directly overlap with the
areas of administration of some of the most important departments in government. Probably the most useful by-prod-
ucts of the task force approach were the involvement of numerous individuals in a study of the problems, thus furthering aims of public education on the issues.

COUNCIL

The second actor of importance to the government departments is the City Council. All government programs involving major expenditures of funds have to be shepherded past
its watchful eyes. While it does not have the power to amend
or add to programs, it does have the right to cut or to block.
The possibility that Council will oppose any given program,
or part of a program, may thus be a powerful influence in
what kind of program is presented to it. Public servants rap-
idly become knowledgeable about the idiosyncracies of each
Council and govern their actions accordingly.

Without exception, informants reported that Baltimore's
City Council was conservative. Occasionally it was described
as a haven of reaction, although individual Council members were singled out for praise. However, Council, though
rejecting a few, has in fact approved a large number of CAA
appropriations. How many additional programs were
dropped before they came to Council as a consequence of
self-censorship is not clear. Officials conceded there had been
some.

At the time the study was being done (Summer 1967)
there were twenty Councillors, with one vacancy. All twenty
were Democrats. It is generally understood that there are
two "factions" in Council, a Pollack-Reed faction and a
D'Alesandro-Schaeffer faction, but the division appears not
to be a very rigid one, particularly in relation to the voting

record of Councillors on civil rights questions. The factions are rather in the nature of coalitions based on pockets of political power, what one observer irreverently termed "fiefdoms," one of the principal purposes of which is to determine alliances during elections. Roughly, the two factions correspond to liberal-conservative divisions in Council, though the ideological bases of the divisions seem not to be very clear or fixed.

Baltimore City Council, as is universally the case with City Councils, takes its role of safeguarding the taxpayer's interests seriously. It tends to reflect the concerns of the principal taxpayers—property owners, entrepreneurs, professional men—above all else. The very poor and the very rich have a small voice in its affairs; the very poor through lack of power, the very rich because more effective means of safeguarding their interests are available to them. Thus, it was reported that large landlords—including slumlords—have spokesmen within Council. During the Public Accommodations controversy, several Councilmen spoke for the position of the saloon-keepers. Ethnic groups are well represented. There are, in addition, two Negro councilmen (Baltimore's population is now close to 50 per cent Negro). One of them is a prominent businessman with a strong political base who has taken consistent civil rights stands. The other draws on weaker support and has had a somewhat more ambiguous voting record. The Negro group, among whom the most acute poverty is to be found, are very noticeably under-represented. Other segments of the community among whom strong anti-Negro prejudice exists are over-represented.

The consequence of a comparatively weak Mayor's office, combined with a Council whose concerns have most closely paralleled those of the most conservative elements of the business community, over a period of many years, has been to discourage active departmental concern with the problems of the Inner City, or the development of radical or far-reaching programs. The consequences are evident in the form of a decaying school system, inadequate welfare services, and in the poverty of other services such as police protection, sanitation, housing, and so on, none of which have developed to meet the spiraling needs of the Inner City. The CAA itself has not been greatly hamstrung, partly because it enjoyed the support of the Mayor, several powerful Councilmen, and influential voices in the community at large, and partly because it is to such a considerable extent funded by the federal government. But from the point of view of the proportion of the city's budget that it receives, the CAA is a comparatively small agency; the true index of the Council's concern is to be found in the spending of all the departments considered together.

THE BUSINESS COMMUNITY

The senior members of the business community are not directly implicated in the hurly-burly of Council politics, although links between the political parties and well-to-do businessmen in the form of campaign contributions are probably as much a part of the Baltimore tradition as is the case in other cities. The absence of their voice in Council does not imply inactivity in influencing civic affairs. Among businessmen's associations which are effective in exercising influence in political affairs—the Chamber of Commerce, the Committee for Downtown, the Voluntary Council (formerly the Thursday Morning Breakfast Club), and the Greater Baltimore Committee—the Greater Baltimore Committee has been most interventionist in its policies. Set up in the 1950s and modeled after Pittsburgh's Allegheny Conference, its membership consists of one hundred of the most influential business leaders in Baltimore. A look at its activities demonstrates its salience to government activities. It was deeply involved in and the moving force behind the development of the Charles Center project, a complex of modern offices, stores, and a Center for Performing Arts, which was undertaken to bring life back into the decaying central business district. This project, which cost in all twenty-five million dollars, was originally funded within the city, though in the end the federal government contributed some thirteen million of the total. The Committee worked closely with the Mayor and President of the City Council in the planning of that development. Another major step in which the Greater Baltimore Committee cooperated with the city's elected officials was the initiation of the Inner Harbour project, which will rejuvenate the city's port facilities.

Both the Charles Center and the Inner Harbour projects are calculated to result in significant benefits to the business community as a whole. But the Greater Baltimore Committee's activities have also taken them into other concerns more closely related to the anti-poverty program and other areas of city government. A joint report of the GBC and the Committee for Downtown on the subject of rapid transit recommended the establishment of more effective communications between the Planning Commission and the Metro Transit Authority. GBC has promoted the creation of a large park around the Jones Falls Expressway, thus coming into conflict with the Economic Development Commission and influential members of the City Council. They were active in the development of a major wholesale food center on the outer ring of the city. They have commented on the problems of Inner City residents obtaining and getting transportation to employment opportunities in outer areas. They gave public support for a proposed open housing ordinance. Efforts to strengthen building code enforcement met City Council opposition and probably foundered on powerful opposition from landlords. GBC has set up a non-profit housing corporation for which they raised upwards of a half-million dollars among their members to take advantage of 221 (d)(3) federal loan money. One of the objects of this program is to "promote the use of new governmental and private development techniques" in the area of low-middle income housing. The directors of the Housing Development Corporation include nine Greater Baltimore Committee members, four from community organizations, plus representatives of the Mayor, City Council, the Planning Commission, and BURHA. Finally, GBC began looking into the problems of neighborhood development some years ago and in the spring of 1967 received $450,000 from OEO for a Model Urban Neighborhood Demonstration, in which a further attempt will be made to involve private industry in the problems of the slums. The largest slice of this allotment will be turned over to the Westinghouse Corporation's system analysis division, in an attempt to develop sophisticated long-term planning. A smaller sum will go directly into a selected neighborhood to begin the process of developing indigenous leadership.

The Committee's vigorous activities and direct intervention in city affairs led one councilman to refer to the GBC as "a government within a government." Clearly in several domains its activities parallel those of city agencies such as the Planning Commission, BURHA and the CAA, and the GBC has the advantage of not being encumbered by City Council restraints to the same degree. On the whole, however, less friction than might be anticipated seems to have resulted, possibly because of the active efforts at communication between GBC and the Mayor and other selected individuals. Of course, the chairmen of the Planning Commission and BURHA are themselves drawn from the business community. In July of this summer (1967) GBC announced the formation of a committee to develop a long range plan for public education, under the chairmanship of Walter Sondheim, who contributed actively to the creation of the CAA. Thus, city departments will continue to be conscious of the influence of the GBC, which has demonstrated that it possesses and will exert influence over the setting of city-wide policy.

The GBC is not the only voice of business. The Committee for Downtown in some sense parallels its concerns and activities. The Chamber of Commerce with its wider membership and looser bonds of association pursues traditional business promotion activities, although it has sporadically become involved in some activities associated with the problems of poverty. This summer, for example, it provided facilities and staff for an emergency program to find jobs for Negroes, in which business loaned some of its people for a period of time. The other body which has concerned itself directly with problems of poverty is the Voluntary Council. The Council which began as the Thursday Morning Club, is made up of a small group of presidents of companies (reportedly controlling 60 per cent of employment opportunities in the city) with the avowed aim of achieving integration of the city's employment picture. After attempting to put their own houses in order, they evolved a technique which they termed "teams of two" in an effort to persuade others in the employment field to move toward opening up employment opportunities to Negroes. It was reported that considerable progress has been made in the last three years, although one senior person conceded freely that senior administrative posts still remain closed to Negroes. The Council has also undertaken some limited experiments with training the unemployed to prepare themselves for opportunities which are available. Lately, they have lent their support to the establishment in Baltimore of an Opportunities Industrialization Center, modeled on the Reverend Leon Sullivan's successful Philadelphia plan, which attempts to develop motivation along with skills. Baltimore's OIC will receive some of the funds of the Concentrated Employment Plan, thus bringing it into close relations with the CAA and the Maryland State Employment Service. Some conflicts of

aim and styles appear to have been the result, although the
program is so new to Baltimore that it is hard to find informants with detached viewpoints to offer. One thing is
clear: city departments in the past have had little to do with
employment problems, and the inevitable increased concern
with the high level of unemployment in slum areas will lead
to new problems of coordination between government and
business. The process begins from a comparatively low level
of mutual trust by the two parties; in particular, business informants unanimously appear to regard the State Employment Service as bureaucratic and inefficient and unaware of
business needs. Their attitudes toward governmental initiatives to date are tinged with skepticism, but at this point
they appear unprepared to undertake a comprehensive program themselves. Though the OIC seems impressive, it lacks
anything like the requisite resources to handle the job.

The brief sketch given here is far from comprehensive.
Members of the business community frequently enjoy no little political power in their own right, quite apart from any
of the business associations. They are drawn, as individuals,
into a multitude of public positions at the city, state, and
federal level. A Mayor who aspires to get things done in a
large way may, on occasion, find it more expedient to ally
himself with kindred spirits in the business community
rather than attempt to mobilize the resources of his city departments and nurse his program through the Council. Senior government officers in some departments find both allies
and opponents in the business community. The Baltimore
"establishment" itself reflects a spectrum of social and political positions, from the activist GBC to the ultra-conservative
Efficiency and Economy Commission. The chairman of the
CAA is a member of the Greater Baltimore Committee. The
principal newspaper in the city is owned by one of the "old"
wealthy Baltimore families. The chairman of the GBC's Education Study Commission is a former chairman of both

BURHA and the School Board. With access to so many ways to exercise influence in the city, the establishment can afford to treat mere "politicians" with a measure of contempt.

The prevailing impression received from informants was that the business community in Baltimore had been for many years ultra-conservative, and had allowed the central business district to deteriorate unchecked. It is possible that with the Greater Baltimore Committee's dynamism the pattern has been permanently reversed, and the flight of business from the center city checked. That, at least, is the avowed aim of the GBC.

VOLUNTARY ASSOCIATIONS

Another segment of the community overlaps with departmental responsibilities. This is the cluster of associations who have traditionally concerned themselves with charitable or welfare activities, and in a broader perspective have felt a responsibility for the setting of the city's social goals. In this area, as in others, a great deal was traditionally left to private initiative, and the Department of Public Welfare represented only one of a number of agencies offering services to the unfortunate and the poor. Within the perspective of a healthy thriving community this policy may well have been effective; the capabilities of the total welfare system cannot hope to keep abreast of the needs of the present poverty population.

The principal centers of power, authority, and influence in the welfare field are the Community Chest, the Associated Jewish Charities, and the Archdiocese of Baltimore. In addition, these three agencies contribute, along with the city and the state, to the support of the Health & Welfare Council (HWC). The Council, more than any other group, attempts to consider the community in the perspective of its total welfare needs. It was, for example, the agency which initiated

and took the leadership in developing the Plan for Action
which led to the CAA. It undertakes, for other agencies including departments of government, experimental programs
which, if they are successful, HWC hopes to turn over to the
permanent line agencies. In 1961, for example, BURHA
turned to the Council to administer an experimental relocation demonstration project. The project was designed with
the intent that a number of departments would release personnel to a task force which would canvass an area about to
be emptied for an urban renewal project which was planned.
In principle, all individuals affected would be visited more
than once in their homes; individual and family problems
would be treated in depth, utilizing the full range of the
city's services; and areas where residents were to be relocated
would be prepared in advance for the newcomers. In practice, the project fell far short of its objectives for a variety of
reasons, the most important of which seems to have been departmental reluctance to release workers to it. It did, however, provide the prototype of the neighborhood centers
which are a basic element in the CAA operations.

Recently, again, the Health & Welfare Council accepted
the responsibility for designing a self-help housing program,
in co-operation with the CAA. An experienced social worker
on contract to the Council worked for some months with a
group of Action Area residents to develop a full-fledged proposal, which after some difficulty was passed by Council. The
Council has also operated a demonstration project, originally in conjunction with the Youth Council, for OEO in
the area of unemployment, called the Job Corps program.
This program which has shown considerable promise, has
not yet found sponsorship from any line agency, and the
Council is feeling restive about taking it past the experimental stage. In this case, the Council's freedom to move quickly
undoubtedly prompted OEO sponsorship, since the laborious

business of getting the program past City Council could be circumvented.

The Health & Welfare Council, with its comparative freedom of movement and its predilection for experimental ideas, offers a place for departmental officials to get programs tested, although its lack of authority to follow through has left more than one promising initiative to wither on the vine. The Council has numerous ties with both "establishments" of the city, governmental and business, as well as with voluntary associations and liberal individuals.

The voluntary associations are themselves linked back informally to such bodies as the Greater Baltimore Committee. The Community Chest receives a million dollars of its funds from Bethlehem Steel alone, although it appears the officials of that company make little use of their potential influence. Several of the directors of the Community Chest are also members of the GBC, though their position on the Chest appears to be more conservative than is evidenced by the GBC. The Chest has several links with the CAA. It was one of the original sponsors of that agency. It has supported its legal aid program among others; but its Board failed to support the CAA's need for funds. At the same time, it was reported that there had been friction in some of its relationships with the new department of government, as might have been anticipated with two agencies which have overlapping responsibilities. The Associated Jewish Charities similarly have numerous links with other elements in the system. Jewish businessmen have been among the most liberal and active members in the GBC, in the various boards and commissions and elsewhere. They also support and influence the Jewish charities. After some hesitation, the Board of the Associated Jewish Charities approved a plan this year which will authorize the setting up of a development corporation to attack the problems of a six square mile area with 50 per cent Jewish

population. The area chosen is presently undergoing a
steady demographic shift with the white population moving
to the city's periphery and to the suburban counties, while
Negroes flood in from the Inner City area. The development
corporation will attempt to arrest this drift by concentrating
municipal services, interesting housing developers in putting
up private investment, and by community organization techniques. In this enterprise the Jewish Charities will share the
leadership with the Archdiocese. Various departments and
city agencies, including the CAA, will also be involved, if
only in an advisory capacity.

The Archdiocese is also becoming concerned in a number
of ways with the problems of the Inner City. Under the leadership of Cardinal Shehan, who has publicly declared himself for civil rights, the Archdiocese is becoming involved in
a low-cost housing project in the new city of Columbia. At
the same time the Catholic hierarchy is considering a plan to
levy special tax on the richer parishes to support work in the
Inner City.

SUMMARY

The departments and agencies of the government of Baltimore City are organized along conventional lines according
to standard bureaucratic principles. Their purpose historically has been to provide a necessary infra-structure of services to permit the free play of forces in an economically and
socially pluralistic type of society. The non-public part of
that society developed a number of organizations, which in
turn were inter-related in a number of ways with the government system. The private sector had what might loosely be
termed an "establishment" with several centers of influence
(educational, professional, industrial, commercial, "old Baltimore," etc.). The middle levels of the community traditionally found representation through a variety of organiza-

tions, including the Chamber of Commerce, religious bodies, City Council, and so on. The lower strata of this traditional society appear to have been less well represented, but nevertheless were partially integrated into the total system, through job patterns, church membership, support for political figures, etc. Thus, whatever one's opinion of the system, as such, it would appear incontestable that there was such a system and one in which all elements of the community were integrated in one fashion or another. The government departments functioned as an integral part of that system, and its concerns were intimately intertwined with the other actors and events of it.

Baltimore's present problem would appear to be that the demographic bases of the traditional system have weakened. Large numbers of individuals have fled the city, and their places taken by economically deprived Negroes. Population changes, however, were not accompanied by commensurate changes in the composition of actors in the system. In part, this may have been the result of lack of knowledge by Negroes of how to manipulate the system. For the most part, however, the evidence supports the hypothesis that the phenomenon has been due to deliberate exclusion of Negroes from positions of power and influence. Thus, it was reliably reported that as recently as three years ago, Negroes were excluded from office jobs in commercial establishments. They continue to be excluded from executive positions in numerous areas. Until fairly recently they received unfavorable consideration for many kinds of government posts. While policy now appears to have changed, qualified Negro candidates for senior posts are naturally not significantly available. Representation through the political process has been, until very recently, limited to tokenism; indeed, it was reported that in the pre-primary maneuvering in 1967, considerable pressure was exerted to prevent a Negro from being included on the majority party's ticket for city-wide office.

Representation through Negro organizations exists—the In-
ter-ministerial Conference, NAACP, CORE, the Urban
League, U-JOIN, etc.—but these organizations are small,
highly competitive, and have restricted access to the centers
of decision-making in the system.

The Community Action Program in Baltimore City, 1965-67

MORTON S. BARATZ

I. ORIGIN AND EVOLUTION

Introduction

Multicomponent welfare programs have operated in Baltimore for many years. Among the oldest are those run by the city's Department of Public Welfare and Department of Health. Equally well established are the many-sided efforts conducted under the auspices of three private organizations, the Archdiocese of Baltimore, the Community Chest, and the Associated Jewish Charities. And for nearly a decade before the Community Action Program (CAP) was formally constituted, the Baltimore Urban Renewal and Housing Agency had been carrying on a CAP-type effort, including community organization and neighborhood development, in its public-housing projects.

It misstates only mildly to say that the CAP is the offspring of these precursors. The conceptions upon which the former is grounded were to a substantial extent distilled from the experience of the latter. In particular, the persons most responsible for setting in motion the events that led to the Baltimore CAP's creation did so out of the conviction that the city's "welfare industry" badly needed revitalization and reorganization. Just when they reached this conclusion and how long they nourished their conviction in private is unknown. It is certain, in any event, that they declared themselves publicly on 18 January 1962. That is as good a date as any to mark the inception of the Baltimore CAP.

"A Letter to Ourselves"

The public statement of 18 January 1962 was issued under the auspices of the Health and Welfare Council of the Baltimore Area, Inc. Entitled "A Letter to Ourselves: A Master Plan for Human Development," the document set down some now-familiar criteria for a revised and enlarged program of welfare activity. Such a program, it was asserted, requires "a comprehensive and coordinated approach rather than a piecemeal attack." It "must envision experimentation, integration, self-analysis [sic] and innovation as well as coordination and intensification of existing services." The program must also command "wide community support." And "if real impact upon serious community problems is to be made, the effort must be carried beyond the area and time of a single demonstration."

Given these terms of reference, the Letter identified five broad areas within which specific programs must be defined:

1. Educational and Occupational Services: training of functionally illiterate adults, vocational-skills classes, youth work projects in renewal areas, special program for school drop-outs;

2. Teamwork on a Family-Centered Basis: an experimental family-centered treatment project, co-operative counseling of and service to truants by the Departments of Recreation and Education;

3. Community Organization Efforts: experimental effort in citizen involvement in developing self-help projects, block

organization and/or neighborhood council development, development of settlement-house-type programs to fill an existing gap in such services in Baltimore, a leadership-development program;

4. Programs of Acculturation: program to acquaint school teachers with "the cultural and environmental background of the child as well as the social forces in the community which influence him" and "incorporation of neighborhood improvement as an integral part of the curriculum at all school levels," experimentation in developing and adapting extension-service programs to urban areas, a family-life education program; and

5. Programs of Research: increase knowledge of characteristics, attitudes, interests, and opinions of the population being dealt with, evaluation of the program itself and its component parts.

The Letter dealt only a glancing blow to questions relating to funding of the proposed programs and to the character of the agency that would be responsible for organizing and implementing a program of this kind. Published more than two years before passage of the Economic Opportunity Act of 1964, the Letter made several references to the Ford Foundation as a potential source of money. A brief reference to Associated Agencies of Oakland, California—a consortium of public and voluntary agencies engaged in a coordinated welfare effort—provides the only clue to the Letter-writers' thinking on structural matters.

In the event, the proposals embodied in the Letter were submitted to the Ford Foundation. The Foundation declined to give support, perhaps because its "gray areas" program was already fully subscribed. Defeated but unbowed, the Health and Welfare Council, in its role of sponsoring agency, turned to local sources. In this effort it was successful: a total of $30,000 was raised—$5000 each from the Community Chest, the Archdiocese of Baltimore, and the Asso-

ciated Jewish Charities, and $15,000 from the City of Balti-
more—to finance translation of the proposals in "A Letter to
Ourselves" into a detailed plan for action. Formal responsibility for preparation of the plan was vested in a Steering
Committee on Human Renewal, comprised of seven persons,
one from each private association that contributed money,
one from the Health and Welfare Council, and three representatives of the Mayor. The Committee was fortified, in
form if not in fact, by six panels, comprised of individuals—
many of them heads of public, quasi-public and voluntary
associations—who were actively engaged in managing various
community programs.

"A Letter to Baltimore from Classroom Teachers"
In May 1964, while the Steering Committee was still at
work, the Baltimore Teachers' Union (AFL-CIO) published
a 17-page document calling for "a dynamic change in educational method and practice." Openly patterned after the cel-
ebrated program of Community Progress, Inc., in New
Haven, Connecticut, the scheme proposed by the teachers'
group called for sixteen changes in Baltimore's educational
effort.[1] The principal points were:

> 1. The establishment of a special category of teachers
> who will meet additional requirements as sociology special-
> ists . . .
> 2. A training course for this special category of teach-
> ers . . .
> 4. Elementary schools should become community centers,
> open twelve hours a day with adult programs in the after-
> noon and evening, and all educational, medical, recrea-
> tional, and social services radiating from the school center
> into the community.
> 5. A building program must be inaugurated immediately

1. Significantly, prior to coming to Baltimore in 1965, the incumbent Super-
intendent of Education held a similar post in New Haven.

to make the physical plant of each inner city school meet the same standards as schools on the periphery of the city . . .

6. The present intelligence tests used in Baltimore must be abolished since they do not provide a valid measure of the abilities of the children of poverty.

7. A program for the revision of text books and visual aids must be put in operation to give recognition to minority groups and to provide material in accord with children's experience.

8. Reading specialists must be assigned to each school.

9. Remedial reading instruction must be provided in classes of six or seven pupils.

10. Class size should be studied with a view toward reduction in present size of classes of inner city children.

11. A program for early identification of disturbed children must be established so that they can get necessary help in the first, second, or third grade.

12. A program for early identification of health problems must be established with provision for supplying glasses, hearing aids, and other equipment necessary for healthful school activity.

13. The program of early admissions must be expanded to include all children who need this service.

14. A program of enrichment such as Higher Horizons must be established in inner city schools.

15. A program to work within the school must be established to give paying jobs to children in need.

16. A program of counseling must be provided in inner city schools from the earliest grade, maintained on a sustained basis throughout the school year.

While the Steering Committee's final product (see below) contained many of the suggestions offered by the Teachers Union, the Committee may well have arrived at its conclusions independently. In other words, it is impossible to determine *ex post facto* what effect the Teachers Union had, if any.

It is clear, however, that the Steering Committee was profoundly influenced by the passage of the Economic Opportunity Act of 1964. Public Law 88-452 was enacted in August. The Plan for Action, which was published in November, not only embodied all the essential elements of a full-
blown CAP, but in places explicitly referred to the EOA.

The Plan for Action

The Steering Committee identified nine tasks ("objectives")
it was to accomplish: designation of an Action Area to receive priority attention; division of the Action Area into
smaller parts for administrative purposes; identification of
specific social problems in the Action Area for the purpose of
determining what welfare programs were required; involvement in the planning process of the heads of public and voluntary groups concerned with health, education, and welfare
in Baltimore City; solicitation of advice from all persons
providing services of all kinds in the Action Area; determination of the perceptions of the Action Area residents concerning their problems and how to solve them; review program experience, especially experimental programs, in other
cities; acquire information on available outside help in implementing the Plan; and develop detailed plans for each of
the services to be provided.

By any reasonable standard, the Steering Committee performed these tasks remarkably well, in light especially of the
tight financial constraints put upon it. Using Census data for
1960, supplemented by historical materials, on-site inspec-
tions, and information supplied by knowledgeable persons, it
carefully delineated an Action Area. It then commissioned a
private firm to do a survey of Action Area residents, thereby
getting current information on incomes, employment status,
educational level, housing characteristics, attitudes, and
opinions. Program proposals were compiled from a number
of sources, including the planning staff, various public and

private organizations in the city, and reports from other cities.

The heart of the Plan for Action was, of course, the package of projects recommended for adoption. Numbering 25 in all and priced in aggregate at nearly $24 million, they were as follows:

1. Community Action for Neighborhood Development and Organization
2. Educational Programs for Professional Assistants and Aides
3. Volunteer Service Corps
4. Library Services
5. Day Care for Pre-school and Young School-Age Children
6. Comprehensive Homemaker Services
7. Maternal and Child-Health Services
8. Street-Club Program
9. Character-Building Youth Services
10. Consumer Protection Program
11. Legal-Services Program
12. Manpower Training Program for Youth and Adults
13. Broadening Horizons through TV
14. Early School-Admissions Program
15. After-School Study and Tutoring Program
16. Summer Program—Enrichment and Remedial
17. Sex Education for Special-Curriculum Pupils
18. Special Reading Programs—Elementary and Secondary
19. Supplemental Teaching Service—Elementary
20. Team-Teaching Organization
21. Educational Work Assignments
22. School-Aide Program
23. Neighborhood Youth Corps
24. Vocationally Oriented Curriculum for Youth with Special Needs
25. Program of Pre-Service Education and Teacher Recruitment, Retention and Retraining for Inner-City Schools

The Steering Committee left no room for doubt that the

key element in this diverse basket of projects was the one at the top of the list, which—in consonance with current fashion—had a catchy acronym, CANDO. The direct precursor of the Community Action Agency of Baltimore, CANDO's role and purposes were to oversee the implementation of the Human Renewal Program, and to synchronize and expedite delivery of various services to the poverty population. CANDO's sole operating arm was to be the Neighborhood Development Program. The latter was seen as the broker or intermediary between the Action Area residents and the institutions engaged in supplying services. It would seek out those in need of help, especially "problem families"; it would provide "psychological first-aid"; and it would be the channel through which CANDO would be apprised of the poverty population's preferences with respect to new services and projects.

Unlike "A Letter to Ourselves," the Plan for Action considered in detail the way in which the Human Renewal Program should be organized and administered. Oversight and management of the entire operation were to be vested in a newly created department of the city government, backed by a 14-person governing board made up of the Mayor, President of the City Council, City Comptroller, and 11 others (including one each from candidates presented by the Archdiocese of Baltimore, Associated Jewish Charities, Community Chest, Health and Welfare Council, and School Commission; no mention was made of the groups from which the other six members were to be drawn). The new city department was to have an executive director, two deputies, and a professional advisory subcommittee. The Action Area was to be divided into 119 neighborhoods, each averaging 10 square blocks in area. Each neighborhood was to be assigned a Neighborhood Development counselor, who would be supported by an advisory group of persons providing services to the population (e.g. teacher, policeman, clergyman, political leader, indigenous leaders). Each counselor would also have one non-professional assistant or more, drawn from among the Action-Area population; the assistants would act as trouble-shooters and case-finders, not as problem-solvers. Furthermore, every neighborhood was to have a Development Center, which would serve both as an office and a neighborhood gathering place. Within the center round-the-clock service was to be provided the residents, with the chief goal of promoting organized self-help efforts and mutual support. The Plan carefully stated that, "It is not intended that [neighborhood] groups engage in aggressive social action."

By and large, the Plan for Action followed the course charted in "A Letter to Ourselves." Both proposed a variety of projects to meet the varied needs of the poverty population. Both proposed experimentation in project design and stressed the need for co-ordination of new and existing projects and services. Both assumed the necessity for wide community support of the anti-poverty effort.

On two points, however, the Plan and the Letter tended to differ. Where the Letter seemed to lean toward private management of the Human Renewal Program, the Plan flatly declared for a governmental agency. Very likely, the position taken on the question by those who drafted the Letter reflected their belief that the needed non-local funds could only be obtained from a private foundation, which would be unwilling to make a direct grant to a municipal government. The Steering Committee is said to have made its choice on a different ground. According to an informed person, the Committee concluded that, given a deep political cleavage within the City Council and given that the Council would demand a large voice in anti-poverty policy-making in return for its financial support (10% of total outlays) of the Human Renewal Program, there would be no program in Baltimore unless it were an integral part of the city government.

The other point on which the Letter and the Plan differed

was that the former stressed, while the latter muted, the need for "a comprehensive and coordinated approach rather than a piecemeal attack." The clear implication in the Letter was that the Human Renewal Program was to be the instrument for comprehensive community-action planning, the framework for making program decisions based on a balancing of anti-poverty needs and resources. Neither explicitly nor implicitly does the Plan reflect this point of view. To the contrary, apart from a few brief and vague references to the need for synchronizing and expediting the delivery of services, the document conveys unmistakably a conception of the Human Renewal Program mainly as a supplier of welfare services, rather than a mechanism for determining goals, setting priorities, balancing needs and resources, and co-ordinating operations.

It is not surprising that the Steering Committee conceptualized the Plan the way it did. As was noted earlier, the published version of the Plan was consciously geared to the provisions of the Economic Opportunity Act of 1964. Because the EOA made no reference whatever to the need for comprehensive planning, the Steering Committee had no particular reason for including that notion in its own design. On the other hand, in order that the Human Renewal Program be eligible for federal grants, the Plan was at pains to meet OEO's requirements, namely, (a) to make "adequate provision for participation in policy-making by the major institutions in the community, both public and private, which have a concern with poverty . . . ," (b) to "demonstrate [CANDO's] ability and intention to mobilize community resources against poverty through the establishment of linkages among and within service systems and through other means," and (c) to obtain "resident participation" in policy formation, and in actual conduct and administration of parts of neighborhood-based programs.

An Alternative Proposal

Two months after the Plan for Action appeared in print and one month before the City Council enacted the ordinance which created the CAA, an "alternative war on poverty plan" was put forward by a private organization calling itself the Union for Jobs or Income Now—acronymically, U-JOIN. Largely personified by a young Negro named Walter Lively, U-JOIN attacked the Human Renewal Program on two closely related grounds: the HRP failed to deal "basically with the most pressing needs of the poor in the city," because it failed to "involve the poor in the formulation of programs that are meaningful to them."

U-JOIN's alternative consisted of four major components: a Community Action Program, a Non-Profit Housing Association, a Neighborhood Job Corps, and a Neighborhood Commons. This set of proposals did not purport to be "a complete program for combating" the problems of the poor. Nor were the poor "involved in any mass scale in drawing up these programs"; but "over five hundred people in the [Action?] area have been approached and their approval was generally enthusiastic as was their criticism of the proposed 'Human Renewal Program.' "

Proposal A, the Community Action Program, provided the political framework for U-JOIN's alternative war-on-poverty plan. U-JOIN left no doubt that Proposal A was the keystone of its scheme: "Since the primary purpose of the Community Action Program is to involve the poor in the formulation of programs that are meaningful to them and since one of the major problems in poor neighborhoods is the lack of organization, it is necessary that the task of organizing these neighborhoods be the *first priority* of the program." (Emphasis in original.) Nor was the poverty population's role in policy-making to be merely advisory: "To guarantee that decision-making will originate with the poor and not with the professionals, there will be a separation between the decision-making structure and the administrative staff *which is subordinate to it*." (Emphasis in original.) Accordingly, the proposed structure called for: (a) neighborhood organizations, which sent representatives to (b) six Area Councils, each of which supplied one representative to (c) The Baltimore Council, a non-profit corporation ruled by a board of 14, consisting of the six area representatives plus the Mayor, President of City Council, City Comptroller, three representatives of previously existing community organizations, and two representatives of trade-union locals with members in the Action Area. In addition, "The anti-poverty board may choose a technical advisory board composed of representatives from various city agencies and private welfare agencies. This advisory board will have no decision-making power."

The scope and functions of each element of the above structure were spelled out in some detail. In brief, the neighborhood organizations, which were to be "based on small functional areas within the Action Area," were to "have the right to *initiate, approve, or veto* projects for their immediate area." (Emphasis in original.) The Area Councils were to make decisions on projects that are too large to be handled by individual Neighborhood Organizations," were to "provide a meeting place for people from different neighborhoods to discuss common problems" and would "coordinate the activities of the Neighborhood Organizations in their Area." The roles of the Baltimore Council were "coordination of the total program," handling projects "that are too large for the Area Councils," initiating new projects that have been ratified at lower levels, preparing financial and progress reports, and applying to City Council and the federal OEO for "funds and assistance."

A sizable full-time staff was to be hired to "advise and expedite the programs of the Community Action structure," including a Coordinator with technical and financial assistants and a corps of community organizers and social-service advisers; "residents of the Action Area should be given preference for all full-time staff jobs." Total costs at full operation were estimated at just under $2.5 million.

Proposal B in the U-JOIN plan was a program "to begin to meet the growing problem of overpriced, rundown housing that plagues this city's low-income communities. Specifically, the program called for "the providing of at least 1000 additional housing units each year . . . either by redeveloping old housing or building new housing that would be made available at low rents or in some way that permits poor families to purchase their homes over a period of years. In addition, this program is designed to provide employment for members of these neighborhoods in the full range of skills involved in construction and to provide an opportunity for on-the-job training in an expanding industry." The estimated median cost per house was fixed at $8000. Total estimated cost of the program was $8.5 million.

Proposal C, the Neighborhood Job Corps, had as its purpose the provision of "work experience, on-the-job training, technical training for young men and women in the Proposed Action Area between the ages of 16 to 24 so that they might be placed in profitable careers. The training jobs would be in various parts of the anti-poverty program, health and welfare services, community groups, government and private agencies." The projected intake of youths was 1000 per year; since no one could remain in the program more than two years, maximum enrollment at any one time would be 2000. Youths not attending school would work 30 hours weekly at a rate of pay not higher than $1.75 per hour; each would be required to spend at least five more hours in "an appropriate educational program," for which he would be compensated at $.50 per hour. In-school youth would work only 15 hours per week at a pay rate not less than $1.25 per hour nor more than $1.75. Total operating expense was estimated at $3.85 million.

The fourth proposed project, Neighborhood Commons, was designed "to utilize the city's vacant lots and dwellings to provide needed community facilities for the residents in the proposed action area." The "commons" might take very different forms: tot-lots, basketball court, a "small, quiet shady cove where the elderly . . . can sit and talk . . ." The project was to be operated by a board made up of professionals and community people, who would hire resident skilled craftsmen to instruct and organize the work of unskilled residents. The maximum expected cost per "commons" was $15,000 and total estimated cost, $1 million.

With its pronounced emphasis on organization and full involvement of the poverty population in the formulation and implementation of anti-poverty programs in Baltimore, the U-JOIN plan differed substantially from its two immediate predecessors, the Letter and the Plan. Moreover, while U-JOIN's proposed projects for housing, employment, skill-training, and recreation had (to a greater degree or less) their counterparts in the Letter to Ourselves or the Plan for Action, the U-JOIN schemes were far more ambitious, both physically and financially. Finally, like its predecessors, U-JOIN expressed little interest in a comprehensive community-action planning process. Indeed, probably as a reflection of its view that most anti-poverty planners were merely pouring old (and inferior) wine into new bottles, U-JOIN refused even to pay lip service to a main principle of the war on poverty, coordination of new and existing welfare services.

The scanty evidence at hand indicates that among the policy-makers in Baltimore there was little sympathy, let alone active support, for U-JOIN's set of proposals. Contrary evidence is unlikely to appear. The sums of money U-JOIN had in mind were huge, relative to what was likely to be made available. Furthermore, U-JOIN's frank insistence that the poor had to be organized and given a major role in policy-making must surely have alarmed the city's establishment. Rare indeed is the person with power, authority or influence who encourages those who threaten his pre-eminence. Beyond that, there were those in the "establishment" who resented U-JOIN's criticisms of existing welfare programs and its implicit characterization of the Plan for Action as an instrument of "welfare colonialism." With three strikes against it, the U-JOIN scheme was "out"—at least for the inning that ended in early 1965.[2]

Ordinance No. 438
On 8 February 1965 the Baltimore City Council ordained "the establishment of a Community Action Agency for the purpose of administering a community action program . . . which will mobilize the resources of the city in order to combat poverty at the neighborhood level and which will be eligible to receive federal aid under the Economic Opportunity Act of 1964 and other relevant federal and state legislation . . ." That the ordinance was designed to enact into law the proposals in the Plan for Action was made clear in the ordinance's preamble: "Whereas, the Mayor and City Council of Baltimore, in cooperation with the Archdiocese of Baltimore, the Associated Jewish Charities, the Community Chest and the Health and Welfare Council, sponsored a study for the purpose of drafting a plan of [sic] action on the problems of Baltimore's disadvantaged people; and Whereas, as a result of this study, a Community Action Program designed to attack the problem at the neighborhood level was drafted . . ." Moreover, the City Coun-

2. This is not to say that U-JOIN was impotent. Largely because of its efforts, a housing program was included in the Plan for Action, and the Plan's employment program was modified.

cil's "Declaration of Policy and Finding of Facts" drew freely on the language in the Plan. One dictum of both Plan and Ordinance particularly stands out: "It is further found that to eliminate the cause of poverty and the problems attendant upon it, it is imperative for the City of Baltimore to engage in a total program of concerted community action which will harness and synchronize its resources for remedial education, job training, health care, environmental improvement, social and physical rehabilitation, and training in home management and healthy family living; such a program, to be effective, must attack the problem at its source, in the neighborhoods."

Also as the Plan for Action proposed, the ordinance created a governing board, dubbed the Community Action Commission (CAC), to "be responsible for the administration and proper operation" of the CAP. But where the Plan (and the Ordinance as it was originally introduced in City Council) called for a governing body of 14 persons, including the principal elected officials in the city and nominees of each of the agencies that financed the Plan's preparation, the ordinance in final form created an 11-member Commission, consisting of a member of the Board of School Commissioners (to be appointed by the Mayor for a one-year term), one member of the City Council (to be elected by the Council for a one-year term), and nine other members (to be appointed by the Mayor for three-year terms). The only formal proviso with respect to the nine "public" members was that "none . . . shall be paid, full time employees of any Federal, State or Municipal department or any private nonprofit health, welfare, or recreation agency, or educational institution." Thus, all of the members of the Steering Committee were eligible to serve, as were residents of the poverty area not employed by a public or voluntary organization providing welfare services. The executive director of the

Health and Welfare Council, a man who played a large role in the drafting of the Plan for Action, was ineligible.

Appointment of an Executive Director and two Associate Directors of CAA was to be vested in the Mayor upon recommendation of the CAC. The tenure of all three professionals was fixed at six years. By its nature, the ordinance laid down general principles rather than specific instructions concerning the powers and duties of the CAC. In doing so, it assumed a posture more nearly akin to that of the Letter to Ourselves than that of the Plan. Most notably, the Commission was "authorized to and shall: (a) Formulate, adopt and implement a *total comprehensive* Community Action Program . . . Such a program would *organize,* coordinate and stimulate existing services . . . In the development of any new project components of the Community Action Program, there shall be maximum feasible participation of the residents of the Action Area or Areas and *all appropriate public and private agencies in both the planning and conducting* of the programs of services to be provided. (b) Evaluate periodically the effectiveness of the project components of the Community Action Program and recommend to the Board of Estimates additions and/or deletions of any such project components." (Emphasis added.) At least at the outset, therefore, the City Council envisioned the CAA and its governing body as, not simply a new enterprise with coordinating functions, but rather the chosen instrument for a thoroughgoing, fully-integrated effort to eradicate poverty in Baltimore.

Organization of the CAC and CAA
As soon as it became clear that a CAP was to be established in Baltimore, the persons and groups whose interests were most vitally affected began a struggle for control over the program and its administering agency. The complexities of this conflict remain to be examined in detail. It does seem

clear, however, that the focal points of conflict in early 1965 were the appointments by the Mayor of CAC members and of CAA's executive director. It is also clear that at least two groups within the city took active roles in the resolution of these issues.

As was observed earlier, the Plan for Action specified that four of the places on the CAC be alloted to nominees of the Plan's four sponsors. Although this prescription was ignored by the City Council, something very much like it continued to be urged upon the Mayor by those concerned. What is more, the coalition of voluntary agencies had two or more nominees for the executive directorship of the CAA. The evidence at hand suggests that each of the persons nominated for appointment to the CAC and the CAA was white.

Therein lay much of the rub. Among the politically active Negroes in Baltimore, especially those who spoke in the name of the blacks in the Action Area, the belief was prevalent that the black community had been largely ignored in the process which produced the Plan for Action. To the Negro leaders, that is to say, the Plan was a program designed by the "white power structure" to do something *for* Negroes. As such, the Plan was suspect.

Unable to shape the Plan to their preferences, the leaders in the Negro community determined to have a loud voice in the way in which the CAP was manned and implemented. To that end, representatives of predominantly Negro groups, notably including U-JOIN, coalesced into the Anti-Poverty Action Committee (APAC). The fray was also entered, independently of APAC, by other prominent Negroes in the city. Their combined efforts, directed mainly at the Mayor and at Councilmen presumed to be friendly or at least neutral, was partially successful. On one hand, despite their vigorous representations, the chairmanship of the CAC was given to a white businessman. On the other hand, the first executive director of CAA was a Negro, although he was not one of those formally endorsed by APAC and its allies. For reasons unrelated to the issues at hand, the initial director resigned soon after he was appointed. By that time, the tenuous bands that held APAC together had given way. Its components, acting independently, uniformly endorsed the candidate who was ultimately appointed.

Negro leaders within and without APAC were also agreed that the majority of members on the CAC should be, as one of them has put it, "committed Negroes," on the ground chiefly that blacks make up 80 per cent of the city's poverty population. This prescription proved difficult to fill. The ordinance debarred appointment of persons employed full-time in the "welfare industry." Many Negroes qualified to sit on the CAC held such jobs.

In due course the Mayor appointed a Commission of six whites and five Negroes. Although three of the latter had been endorsed by persons and groups who had openly opposed the concept of a CAP from the beginning and although none of the 11 appointees was either poverty-stricken or a resident of the Action Area, the appointments were accepted in good grace by all concerned. However, within four months the City Council (under direct pressure from Washington) enacted Ordinance No. 1258, which expanded the CAC from 11 members to 15, to include four representatives of the poor.

Application for Federal Funds
The City of Baltimore filed its application for federal funds under the EOA on 7 December 1964, less than a month after the Plan for Action was published. Understandably, the application was a virtual reprise of the Plan. The only significant difference between the two, in fact, was that no funds were sought for five of the twenty-five components listed in the Plan. The application to OEO noted that two components, Maternal and Child Health Services and the Man-

power Training Program, were already financed. Private financing had already been arranged for Character Building Youth Services. And funds were to be requested later for Broadening Horizons through TV and the Vocationally Oriented Curriculum. The total estimated cost of all component projects was given as $4,651,255. The amount of grant funds requested under Title II-A was $2,059,136.

To judge from the timetable presented to OEO, the Baltimore anti-poverty planners were sanguine over the prospects of getting the CAP off the ground quickly. Ten of the projects would commence supplying services within a month after the application was approved. One would be fully operating within two months. Two neighborhood centers, together with their Library Services, Consumer Protection, and Legal Services components, would be operating within three months. The Day Care projects, both Group and Family, would begin actual operations within four months. On the premise that the application would be approved before 1 January 1965 (itself an optimistic assumption), the summer programs were scheduled to begin within 6 months. All projects would be in full operation at the end of 12 months.

Implementation of the CAP

OEO's initial grant to Baltimore, officially designated as Maryland CAP #207, was approved by Sargent Shriver on 15 February 1965. The federal contribution was to be $1,-871,330, an amount that was $187,806 (roughly 9 per cent) less than that applied for. OEO refused to provide funds for four proposed components. Financing for Training of Inner-City Teachers was "deferred until program specifics are defined and resubmitted for a 207 grant." The project in Sex Education was rejected because it "involves only pupils in the target area." The Team Teaching proposal was turned down because the "program is curricula [sic] in nature and would merely have reduced teachers' normal load." The

School-Aide component was disapproved because "educational programs under this grant have provisions for school aide assistance."

The CAP was launched, therefore, with total resources of $2,079,255, of which $207,925 was to be provided in cash and kind by the City. Little time was wasted in initiating the program. In the chronological order of their formal start, and as briefly described by CAA itself, these projects were implemented:

1. Neighborhood Youth Corps (15 April 1965)—Provides out-of-school and unemployed youth 16–21 years of age with job opportunities created in governmental and private community service agencies; helps form good work habits and attitudes as well as work experience, helps enrollees find realistic direction for their lives, including returning to school, job placement, etc. (Financed by U. S. Department of Labor under Title I-B of EOA.)

2. Consumer Protection (3 May 1965)—Provides a program of consumer education to low-income individuals and groups in the Action Area, with emphasis on budgeting of income and avoidance of exploitation in the market place, in purchasing or renting a home, or in borrowing; awakens area residents to available community resources to assist them on consumer problems confronting them. (Third-party contract with Urban League.)

3. Neighborhood Centers Program (17 June 1965)—Designed to provide professional staff trained in the skills of community organization and neighborhood development in each neighborhood area being served. The focal point of these services in each neighborhood is a Neighborhood Service Center. The NSC is developed within existing facilities in the community and houses the office of the Neighborhood Development Counselor and his assistants. The main purpose of the Neighborhood Center is to serve as a central neighborhood location to which residents can come with

their problems and be put in touch with the appropriate helping resources. In effect, the NSC is designed to become the focal point for individual and neighborhood efforts to overcome poverty.

4. Library Services (17 June 1965)—Promotes fuller utilization of public library resources by having books available in the Centers and mobile units in the Action Area; provides materials in the Action Area to help residents with reading difficulties and to stimulate interest in books; offers help to residents through reading, class visits to the library, programs using films, records, etc.; part of the Neighborhood Center team. (Third-party contract with Enoch Pratt Free Library.)

5. Comprehensive Homemaker Service (1 July 1965)— Makes homemakers readily available to low-income families to reduce the risk of family break-up resulting from serious problems of health and social adjustment; employs personnel, including neighborhood residents, to furnish home help services to families with children, and to convalescent, aged, acutely or chronically ill and disabled persons in order to maintain or help develop a healthy household routine. Emphasis is placed on the variety of social problems confronting the family, and on help to the aged or the chronically ill. (Third-party contract, originally with Department of Public Welfare and Instructional Visiting Nurse Association, but since 1 October 1966 with DPW only.)

6. Volunteer Service Corps (15 July 1965)—Recruits, screens, orients and assigns volunteers to serve residents of the Action Area; volunteer service will be directly through the Neighborhood Centers or through any of the programs offered under third-party contracts; some volunteers may also be working with residents of the Action Area through agencies other than third-party contractors. (Originally a third-party contract with Health and Welfare Council, but since 1 October 1966 handled directly by CAA.)

7. Street Club Program (15 July 1965)—Provides workers to help groups of delinquent and pre-delinquent youth redirect their energies from anti-social to non-destructive behavior; provides a meeting place (rented store front, church building, etc.) which the group can feel is its own; includes athletic contests, games, trips, dances, etc., for both boys and girls. (Third-party contract with Department of Recreation and Parks.)

8. Day-Care Centers (15 August 1965)—Provides a safe and healthy environment for pre-school children during hours of the day when their own parents cannot provide such care; stimulates and encourages positive learning experiences; provides professional guidance on problems of child care; groups will meet in Day Care centers or Neighborhood Centers. (Third-party contract with Department of Public Welfare.)

9. Family Day Care (15 August 1965)—Same as Day-Care Centers, except that care is provided in private homes. (Third-party contract with Department of Public Welfare.)

10. Small Business Development Center (3 January 1966) —To develop opportunities for new business ventures and upgrade the quality of operations of existing ones in order to create additional job opportunities for the city's poor. In addition, it will provide interested persons and groups with information, advice, and counsel concerning small business opportunities and will facilitate their entry into such activities.

11. Knox Day Care (16 March 1966)—Same as Day-Care Centers. (Third-party contract with church group.)

12. Project ENABLE (31 March 1966)—To provide parent education through discussion groups in the areas of child care, education, recreation, and household management. Particular attention will be paid to the fragmented family. (Third-party contract with Urban League and others.)

13. Family Planning (1 July 1966)—Designed to bring birth-control information and services to residents by estab-

lishing branch clinics, providing staff for these clinics, enlisting local residents to assist with patient recruitment and involving community leaders. (Third-party contract with Planned Parenthood association of Maryland.)

14. Legal Services to the Poor (1 September 1966)—Designed to provide an easily accessible legal-consultation service in the Neighborhood Service Centers on a regular schedule. In reference to civil cases, this means free services wherever indicated under the eligibility rules of the Legal Aid Bureau and, in some cases, referrals. In reference to criminal cases, this means that only advice and help in obtaining counsel, either private or court-appointed, would be given.

15. Emergency Services (1 September 1966)—Designed to meet the immediate needs of children and adults in emergent situations arising from lack of food, clothing, shelter, utilities, and from other conditions causing crisis. The program will serve residents in a specified location within the Target Area; services and operational procedures will be extended to include those not now provided in the Welfare program. This program is also designed to develop community involvement through the active participation of existing agencies so that an improved approach to meeting emergencies may be incorporated in existing programs. (Third-party contract with Department of Public Welfare.)

In addition to those listed, the CAP has included two summer programs, Camp Farthest Out and Operation Champ. The former, which functioned during August 1965 under a third-party contract with a private group, in the CAA's words "was designed to provide stimulating cultural experiences along with providing medical services for diagnostic and remedial assistance." Operation Champ functioned in the summer of 1966 under a third-party contract with the Western Police Boys Clubs, Inc. Difficult to categorize, it was "designed for youth between the ages of 16–21 years . . . for the purpose of enhancing a more harmonious relationship between the police and the youth populace through a variety of academic, cultural, recreation, moral, and character building programs."

During its first year the CAA devoted a substantial portion of its CAP grant to educational projects. Under a third-party contract with the Baltimore Department of Education, it financed a project called Educational Work Assignments, the equivalent for in-school youngsters of the Neighborhood Youth Corps. This component continues under CAA sponsorship. CAA also delegated originally to the Department of Education the responsibility for administering the educational projects proposed in the Plan for Action: enrichment, early-school admissions, remedial, after-school study and tutoring, special reading, supplemental teaching, and educational-program development. Except for the last-named, all have been terminated as CAP components, chiefly because the Department of Education is now able to carry on similar activities on a much larger scale with funds appropriated by the Congress under the Elementary and Secondary Education Act of 1965. Also now terminated is an educational project for professional assistants and aides, originally delegated by CAA to Baltimore Junior College.

Although CAA no longer finances pre-school projects of the Department of Education, it continues to support efforts along those lines during the summer months. In the summer of 1966, for instance, it awarded 10 contracts, 9 to church-related institutions and one to a state college, for projects similar to that run in August 1965 by Camp Farthest Out, Inc.

Rounding out the list of ongoing components is Program Development. Administered under a third-party contract by the Health and Welfare Council, this project involves screening of all proposals to CAA (except those concerned with schooling and day-care centers) and co-ordinating those that seem closely related to one another.

At the close of 1966 some 19 proposals were awaiting action by the CAC. Three warrant brief description. Although skill-training and employment are key elements of the over-all anti-poverty effort, development of a training-apprentice-ship system has received relatively little emphasis in the Baltimore CAP. As a prior step toward filling this gap in the program, CAA has recommended that funds be authorized for hiring four staff assistants who would be charged with de-vising a plan for manpower development. A second pending (and very controversial) proposal is to create a CAP Man-power-Recruiting and Training Division. Envisaged as a non-profit, corporate subsidiary of the CAA, it would pro-vide the agency with services now performed for it by the Baltimore Civil Service Commission. Specifically, the functions of the Manpower Corporation would be "to actively seek out potential candidates for Community Action Agency posi-tions, to provide whatever testing procedures may be re-quired, and to provide quickly staff required to operate the Community Action Program." Recruits would be paid by the Manpower Corporation and assigned to CAA. Directors of the Corporation would be representatives of public and private personnel agencies, Action-Area residents, the CAC, and the "business community."

The most controversial of the pending projects is one called Self-Help-Housing. Conceived by a group of Action-Area residents styling themselves the Neighborhood Housing Action Committee and endorsed by the Health and Welfare Council (which provided a staff member to work with NHAC), the proposal bears some resemblance to the ambi-tious but ill-fated project of U-JOIN, described earlier. The pending proposal "is intended to provide a self-help mecha-nism by which Action Area residents can take responsibility for services to expedite and supplement existing City Serv-ices to improve housing and environmental conditions." To be administered by a non-profit corporation controlled by the poverty population, the project features an Environmental Improvement Service that would employ residents "to supplement and facilitate the sanitation and environmental health services of the City agencies"; housing advisory services to furnish residents with "information, education and counseling in matters relating to housing," and to refer them to "needed services to improve housing"; mediation panels for tenant-landlord disputes and a house-finding service for all those "who wish to move for any legitimate reason"; and a tool pool and materials service "where tenants and resident owners . . . may borrow tools and secure materials which can be applied by unskilled labor . . . for minor repairs which are not regulated by City code."

For the fiscal year ending 30 June 1967 the CAP has an approved federal budget of $6,885,228. As can be seen in Table I, almost one-fourth of that sum is earmarked for Neighborhood Services and another 36 per cent for the Neighborhood Youth Corps and Educational Work Assignments. The remainder is divided in comparatively small amounts among 18 other components.

II. CURRENT CHARACTER OF CAP

Intended Output

In principle, a CAP can be designed to serve one or a combination of six broad functions. It could focus on mobilization of resources. It could fill gaps in the existing package of anti-poverty projects, offering services not heretofore supplied. It could direct its energies to innovation in the production and delivery of services, i.e. finding new ways to achieve goals. A fourth possibility is to lay heaviest stress on rationalizing the anti-poverty effort by promoting more coordination among agencies in the planning and actual distribution of services. Fifth, it could serve as an irritant or "needler," in the interest of bringing about changes in established structures and processes through either changes in leg-

Table I. Approved Federal Budget for CAP Components
Fiscal Year 1967

PROGRAM	APPROVED FEDERAL BUDGET	PER CENT OF TOTAL
Administrative Direction and Control	$420,835	6.1
Comprehensive Homemaker-DPW (July to Sept. '66)	18,981	0.3
Comprehensive Homemaker-IVNA (July to Sept. '66)	14,108	0.2
Comprehensive Homemaker-DPW (Oct. to June '67)	127,561	1.9
Consumer Protection	76,519	1.2
Day Care—Centers (Sept. to June '67)	337,826	4.9
Day Care—Family	242,337	3.5
Educational Work Assignments (July & Aug. '66)	522,132	7.6
Educational Work Assignments (Sept. to June '67)	572,680	8.3
Emergency Services (Sept. to June '67)	100,536	1.5
Family Planning (Dec. to June '67)	69,976	1.0
Headstart (July & Aug. '66)	151,918	2.2
Knox Day Care	78,566	1.1
Legal Services to the Poor	259,919	3.8
Library Services	182,400	2.6
Neighborhood Services	1,567,229	22.7
Neighborhood Youth Corps (July to Oct. 20, '66)	401,169	5.8
Neighborhood Youth Corps (Oct. 21, '66 to June '67)	1,018,358	14.7
Operation Champ (July to Oct. 15, '66)	87,640	1.3
Program Development & Evaluation—H & W	11,350	0.2
Project Enable (July '66 to March '67)	52,063	0.8
Self-Help Housing	226,362	3.3
Small Business Development Center	116,429	1.7
Street Club	205,730	3.0
Volunteer Service Corps—H & W (July to Sept. '66)	6,810	0.1
Volunteer Service Corps—CAA (Oct. '66 to June '67)	15,794	0.2
TOTAL	$6,885,228	100.0

islation or in administrative regulations. Finally, the CAP's sole or main thrust could be toward organizing the poverty population, developing indigenous leadership, and encouraging it to take a larger role in community decision-making.

The Baltimore CAP seeks, to a greater degree or less, to do most of these things. The Emergency Services, Consumer Protection, and Day-Care components, among others, have filled gaps in the pre-existing output mix of the "anti-poverty industry" in Baltimore. The Neighborhood Services project is a potentially significant innovation. Several attempts, some more fruitful than others, have been made at coordination at all levels of the anti-poverty industry in the city. CAA and its constituent elements have done some needling. And a substantial amount of resources has already been committed to enlargement of the social and political role of the poverty population.

While the policy-makers in the CAA try to play a variety of roles, they have not yet consciously decided the priority to be assigned to each. Among members of the agency staff there are, understandably, differing views as to the central purpose of CAP. None of the positions taken commands a majority. The Community Action Commissioners have become increasingly aware that criteria upon which to base hard choices must be established. Until recently, the need to make such choices has been obscured by the more mundane problems attendant upon the creation of a new agency. Now, however, CAA is a going concern. What is more important, it seems virtually certain that some of the appropriations for the CAP will be cut in the near future, as a result of which there will be much less room for compromises that avoid rather than cope with the question of priorities.

Organization of the CAP

As a department of the city government, the CAA is subject to direct and continuing supervision by the Mayor, City Council, and Board of Estimates. The agency is, therefore, fully exposed to the changing political winds. Beyond that, it has only limited power and authority to effect important changes in anti-poverty policy. It is but one of a number of municipal departments with anti-poverty responsibilities; and as a new institution it lacks prestige and a constituency that commands respect in the community political system. As a result, CAA must choose its goals with more care than would a private agency and must pursue its objectives more gingerly.

The main redeeming feature of the Baltimore arrangement is that as a governmental institution, CAA cannot be ignored when other public bodies consider anti-poverty policy. CAA is part of the "establishment," and as such is paid some deference in the areas of its concern. In brief, then, the CAA is—by comparison with its private counterparts in other cities—unusually constrained in some respects, benefited in others.

One further point must be made in connection with the relationship of the CAA to the city government. In response to the 1966 amendments (Public Law 89-794) to Section 202 of the Economic Opportunity Act of 1964—requiring that at least one-third of the CAC's members be drawn from and elected by the Action-Area population—the CAA staff drafted a plan for greater involvement of the poverty group in the planning and conduct of the CAP. The draft provided, among other things, that the CAC have a complement of 35 persons, 11 appointed by the Mayor (as was provided in the original ordinance) and the other 24 nominated or elected by the residents of the Action Area, under the following procedure:

In every neighborhood where there is a Neighborhood Development Team, a Neighborhood Council would be established, led by indigenous persons selected by the residents themselves. The Councils, in addition to carrying on various community-organization activities, would designate two representatives to a Target Area Advisory Committee; currently, there are two Target Areas. The Advisory Committees, consisting of a maximum of 20 persons each, would have a role in overall policy planning and—what is more important for present purposes—would constitute a panel of candidates for election to the CAC. Specifically, in yearly elections among the poverty population the 12 individuals on each Advisory Committee receiving the largest number of votes would be elected to CAC for one-year terms.

Whether a Commission of 35 could operate effectively is open to question. It is equally questionable whether the Mayor and City Council would be willing to surrender their voting dominance over an agency with a large claim on the city's financial resources. In any case, the Personnel Committee of the CAC devised its own proposal, one which was more likely to be acceptable to the Mayor and Council. The CAC's scheme provided that the Commission be enlarged to a membership of 19, 11 appointed by the Mayor and 8 elected by Action Area residents.

To complicate matters further, a committee (elected at an open "convention" in mid-December 1966) of Action-Area residents devised a scheme of their own, calling for a Commission with 29 members. Of these, 24 would be nominated or elected by residents of the poverty areas. The remaining five would be appointed by the Mayor, with the advice and consent of representatives of the poverty population. All indications were that this proposal was less a firm demand than a basis for bargaining.

The issue was ultimately resolved with an agreement that CAC would consist of 21 members, 11 appointed by the Mayor and 10 representing the Action Area.

Programmatic Aspects of CAP

There are several ways of overviewing the component parts of the Baltimore CAP. One has already been suggested, namely, to classify each project in terms of its broad function —mobilization, gap-filling, innovation, co-ordination, irritation, or activation. Another approach is to categorize components by the population sub-group each is aimed at. Still another is to relate projects to specific personal or family deprivations, for example, lack of health, lack of physical comfort,

lack of safety, and so on. And yet another approach is to classify components according to whether they are intended to
relieve present problems or reduce the likelihood of future
difficulties. There is little basis for choice among these possibilities. Each can serve a useful purpose. Each also has limitations, not least of which is that all sub-categories are not
mutually exclusive.

If the CAP is disaggregated in terms of the population
sub-groups to which its individual components are primarily
aimed, it looks as follows:

Components for 0–5-year-olds:
    Day Care
    Head Start
Components for 6–16-year-olds:
    Street Clubs
    Educational Work Assignments
    Library Services
    Operation Champ
Components for 17–21-year-olds:
    Neighborhood Youth Corps
    Family Planning
    Library Services
Components for Adults:
    Emergency Services
    Consumer Protection
    Legal Services
    Project ENABLE
    Family Planning
    Library Services
    Small Business Development Center
    Comprehensive Homemaker Service
Components for All Age Groups:
    Neighborhood Service Centers
    Volunteer Service Corps
    Program Development

A breakdown into "remedial" and "preventive" categories looks this way:

Components Designed To Relieve Current Problems:
  Emergency Services
  Comprehensive Homemaker Service
  Legal Services
  Consumer Protection
  Volunteer Service Corps
  Neighborhood Service Centers
Components Designed To Reduce the Risk of Future Problems:
  Neighborhood Youth Corps
  Educational Work Assignments
  Head Start
  Day Care
  Street Clubs
  Operation Champ
  Family Planning
  Small Business Development Center
  Library Services
  Project ENABLE
  Volunteer Service Corps
  Program Development
  Neighborhood Service Centers

There is no particular sequence in which these activities are to be performed. Nor is there a single "theory" that underlies the CAP; as was suggested earlier, it is a compromise among several theories of social-welfare policy. The Baltimore CAA is perhaps most aptly characterized as one more "firm" in the group of firms that constitute the "anti-poverty industry" in the city. Like its older counterparts, both governmental and voluntary, CAA produces or delivers a variety of problem-focused services, each directed to one selected segment or more of the poverty population. By and large, CAA's package of services complements those supplied by

the other firms. To a limited extent, however, CAA's offer-
ings are competitive: there is partial overlapping, for example, between the community-organization efforts in CAA's
neighborhood centers and BURHA's "shelter-plus" program
in public housing projects.

Developmental Aspects

As Table I makes evident, CAA has committed most of its
resources thus far to production and distribution of services
not previously available to Baltimore's poverty population.
Now faced with the prospect of substantial cuts in its budget,
CAA must make some critical decisions. Should it continue
to spend its scarce resources on specific services? Or should it
concentrate on innovation and co-ordination, spinning off its
service components to established agencies such as the Department of Public Welfare and the Department of Health?
Or should CAA devote all its inputs to political activity
among and on behalf of the poverty group?

   Neither the CAC nor the CAA has yet formulated answers
to these questions, in large part because the undermanned
professional staff has lacked the time. This is not to say that
the CAP is static. Program emphases have shifted in the past
and continue to do so. At this moment, for example, CAA is
about to undertake a large job-training program, financed
by the U.S. Department of Labor. In short, the Baltimore
CAP may be approaching a major turning point. Whether it
will change or how or in what direction is as yet unclear.

III. CAP AND THE POLITICAL SYSTEM

Pending extended research and analysis, it is possible only to
provide a rough sketch of the political system within which
the CAP is shaped and executed. One broad generalization
does seem warranted. The distribution of power in Baltimore is so delicately balanced that no policy changes leading

to a major reallocation of values appears possible at this time.

A number of individuals and groups are pressing for substantial changes via anti-poverty policy. Among them are U-JOIN, CORE, an informal cluster of Negroes prominent in local affairs, a small number of philanthropically inclined whites acting as individuals or as spokesmen for voluntary associations, a few members of the City Council, and certain key figures in the municipal government bureaucracy. Though these individuals and associations sometimes disagree over policy priorities and specific aspects of given policies, they have in common the view that CAP can become the instrument for a major improvement in the economic, political and social status of the poverty population in general and the Negro poor in particular.

The outright opponents of a significant reallocation of values are more difficult to identify. The evidence assembled thus far indicates overt resistance on the part of whites in the lower-middle-income bracket (roughly $3500–$6000 annual income) who live in neighborhoods contiguous to or near the Action Area. Themselves hard-pressed financially, these individuals are resentful over the aid given the poverty group and are fearful that upwardly mobile Negroes will deprive them of their own recently won improvement in status. Resistance to certain types of change is also manifested by some members of the City Council, and by a few key officials in the municipal bureaucracy.

Still apparently on the sidelines are all those persons and groups in Baltimore whose interests have not yet been significantly affected for good or ill by the CAP. Included among the inactive are the bulk of the business community, the trade unions, and the overwhelming majority of the relatively affluent white population.

To a greater degree or less, the City Council reflects all of these cross-currents. Beyond that, the Council—although

made up entirely of Democrats—is split into two factions
which are at odds over a number of issues, of which anti-poverty is only one. The Council, which is the final arbiter on
policy proposals of CAA and CAC, is understandably loath
to antagonize any person or group with actual or potential
power, authority, or influence. With respect to anti-poverty
policy in particular, the Council is steering a very cautious
course, one which to date has kept both proponents and opponents of change sullen, but not mutinous. Thus, the Council has approved CAP components aimed at relieving the
problems of the poor, e.g. emergency services, comprehensive
homemakers service, educational projects. But it vetoed a
plan for voter registration in the Action Area, blocked projects that it feared would bring about mixed occupancy of
presently all-white neighborhoods, and resisted demands that
the poverty population be given greater responsibilities and
privileges in planning and implementing CAP.

By definition, CAA is committed to policies which effect
major changes in the economic, political, and social status of
the Action Area residents. In spite of its very limited budget,
the difficulties involved in launching a new enterprise, a general lack of information on which to base budget-allocation
decisions, and some resistance within City Council to the
basic philosophy of the program, the Agency has made substantial progress. Now that it is a going concern, the question is what role it should evolve for itself in order to meet
its commitment to major change.

The Political Significance of Citizen Participation

PETER BACHRACH, MORTON S. BARATZ, AND MARGARET LEVI

Title II, Section 202(a) of the Economic Opportunity Act of 1964 provides that community action programs must be "developed, conducted, and administered with the maximum feasible participation of residents of the areas and members of the groups served . . ." The proviso is open to a number of interpretations. To some persons, it connotes what has been called grass roots democracy, that is, the taking of an active role in community affairs by every citizen, no matter how mean his condition of life. Implicit in this view is the belief that participation is the chief means by which the poverty-stricken can acquire the power, authority, and influence they need to advance their economic and social status. To others, participation involves a collaborative relationship between those who give and those who receive help, the implication being that if the poor take an active part in decisions about the types and characteristics of the services made available to them they will not only get the kind of help they want, but in the process will be cured of their feelings of social alienation and will acquire a sense of individual worth.

In yet another view, participation connotes involvement in the actual delivery of anti-poverty services, i.e. the poor themselves should serve as homemakers, day-care workers, etc., thereby raising their economic status or self-respect, or both.

Each of these constructions appears to fall within one of two broader conceptions of what citizen participation is and how it contributes to the elimination of poverty. One of the conceptions may be labeled interest-oriented participation, the other cooptative participation. The central premise of this essay is that an analysis of the assumptions, principles, and goals underlying these two differing conceptions will be helpful in developing a framework for an appraisal of: (a) the nature, purpose, and extent of citizen participation in Baltimore's effort to eliminate poverty; (b) whether, if at all, citizen participation among the poor and related groups in Baltimore has been a significant factor in changing the distribution of authority and power within the community as a whole; and (c) the appropriate future role for citizen participation in the ongoing anti-poverty effort.

The discussion that follows begins with an attempt to define citizen participation, without reference to any of its possible objectives. We then examine the character and implications of two specific formulations of the concept. Following this, we consider whether and how each viewpoint can be of value in analyzing and evaluating the scope and impact of programs to increase citizen participation.

CITIZEN PARTICIPATION AS POLITICAL ACTION

A political system is a set of institutions and procedures the "output" of which is an allocation of values recognized as legitimate by the great majority who live within the polity. By extension, anyone who attempts to sustain or to alter the existing authoritative allocation of values is engaging in political action. To the extent, therefore, that citizen participation refers to an effort by one person or more to preserve or change the value-allocation, citizen participation is a form of political action. However, it must be emphasized that the concept of citizen participation is a form of, and not synonymous with, political action; the word *citizen* qualifies participation in that it refers to ordinary men and women, as distinguished from officials and elites, as political participants.

Virtually all forms of citizen participation have as their object the preservation or change of the existing value allocation. Thus, the thrust of some activities is to redistribute power, authority, and influence in favor of the participants; an illustration is participation in the process of decision-making with respect to the nature and size of anti-poverty programs. Other forms of participation center on redistribution of income, and still others seek to bring about a reallocation of such values as respect and affection.

It must be stressed that it is immaterial whether political action in the form of citizen participation is brought to bear upon "private" or "governmental" institutions. Both are integral elements of the political system. What *does* matter is that those in the key centers of decision, "private" or "public," have the authority—the "right" in the eyes of the rest of the community—to make decisions that affect the allocation of values, and that the values being allocated rank high in the preference schemes of a substantial number in the relevant community.

What constitutes the scope of citizen participation? Does the concept encompass *all* political action by non-elites, no matter how indirect to the process of value-allocation their action may be? There is no clear-cut answer to this question. To confine the scope of participation to explicit representation in the shaping and implementing of policies is clearly too narrow, because it excludes such obvious forms of political activity as voting, petitioning for redress of grievances, demonstrating, and participation in the formulation and implementation of policies within political groups and organizations—all of them indirect means of selecting decision-makers or providing decision-makers with policy guidelines. On the other hand, a program that does no more than employ a few citizens in the delivery of services has little or no impact on the allocation of values, thus does not qualify as citizen participation.

Happily, it is not necessary to locate precisely the boundary beyond which citizen participation becomes "too indirect" to be considered political action. The relevant question, instead, is how widely the concept *should* be construed. The answer to this question hinges upon the goals that citizen participation is intended to achieve.

INTEREST-ORIENTED PARTICIPATION

In the minds of many, the central goal of citizen participation should be the achievement by everyone in society of a set of interests that are subject to defense or attainment within the political system and the resources and know-how to promote them. This view is rooted in the democratic principle that each member of society is inherently equal in worth to every other member. In the words of a seventeenth century observer, ". . . the poorest he that is in England hath a life to live as the richest he," and therefore each person ought "to have a voice" in selecting the persons "who make laws for him." Underpinning this view are three fundamental assumptions. The first of them is that political awareness emerges within the consciousness of man when he realizes that he has personal interests to protect and, further, that politics are instrumental in the shaping and determination of his interests. Second, each man is presumed to be the best judge of his own interests. Third, if an individual must choose between courses of action, he is assumed to be the most qualified to decide which course will better serve his interest.[1]

1. This is not to say that the citizen must also participate in all decisions

Out of a theory of politics that encouraged and legitimatized citizen participation as a means of promoting self-interest, there naturally evolved a political system characterized by universal suffrage, periodic elections, contesting political parties, and well-developed and complex interaction among interest groups. This kind of system, as the American experience bears witness, can well serve the interests of most of the citizenry. But it is a system that almost inevitably excludes those in poverty. Comparatively few of the poor have a developed sense of self-interest, much less a confidence that it can be promoted through political action. It is not surprising, therefore, that so many of them take no part in elections or in organized activities.[2] "The flaw in the pluralist heaven," wrote E. E. Schattschneider, "is that the heavenly chorus sings with a strong upper-class accent."[3]

By what means can the impoverished be helped to see the relevance of politics and to utilize the pluralistic political system for their own benefit (following the lead of farmers, laborers, and civil-rights groups, among others)?[4] There are, in principle, many means. Bulking large among them is the anti-poverty program.

involving implementation of his value choices. On technical questions he is likely to lack the special competence that is called for, consequently must yield to the expert.

2. See Angus Campbell, *The American Voter* (New York, 1960), p. 91; Edward Dreyer and Walter Rosenbaum, *Public Opinion & Electoral Behavior* (Belmont, Calif.), and Murray B. Levin, *The Alienated Voter* (New York, 1960).

3. *The Semi-Sovereign People* (New York, 1960), p. 35; also see Julian Woodward and Elmo Roper, "Political Activity of American Citizens," *American Political Science Review* (Dec. 1950), p. 874; and Fred Greenstein *The American Party System & The American People* (New York), pp. 5–17.

4. Writing in an African context, Professor Spiro observes: "In a community whose members are unaware of the possibilities of doing something about their common fate, there is no politics to the extent of this unawareness. The moment, and to the extent, that some members do become aware of the possibility of doing something about their economic welfare, their social structure, their cultural values, or other aspects of their common existence, politics begins—and begins to develop." Herbert Spiro, "The Primacy of Political Development," in H. Spiro (ed.), *Africa* (New York, 1966), p. 153.

Given an interest-oriented conception, therefore, the overriding issue is not whether participation of the poor contributes to the effectiveness of anti-poverty programs. The critical question, rather, is whether the programs can engender among the poor a sense of vested interest in the programs and a growing preparedness to organize and struggle for the introduction, improvement, and enlargement of anti-poverty projects. Stated in other terms, the fundamental premise of the interest-oriented approach to the anti-poverty effort is that, although existing programs are at present woefully insufficient to eliminate poverty, they do provide a basis for the development of a widespread political awakening among the poverty population. The gap between those in poverty and the ongoing political process must be closed. The first step toward this goal is a correct understanding of the relationship between interests and aspirations, on one hand, and on the other, citizen participation. If anti-poverty programs develop and encourage interests and aspirations (as ends to be politically sought after and protected), citizen participation (the means) could very likely grow beyond the strictly governmental structure, reaching ultimately into all parts of the economy and polity. Until this happens, it is much less probable that poverty—seen as a multi-faceted problem, rather than simply as low income—will be significantly reduced.

COOPTATIVE PARTICIPATION [5]

Citizen participation is cooptative in nature when the activities of non-elites in decision-making and policy implementation are channeled toward the pre-conceived goals of higher

5. Cooptation, as a form of participation, is discussed briefly in Arthur Shostak, "Politics, Poverty and Problems," Address to Eastern Sociological Society, Spring 1966 (mimeo.), p. 3 and *passim*.

authorities. From the latter's standpoint, the objective of cooptative participation is to evoke the participants' interest, enthusiasm, and sense of identity with the goals of the enterprise in question. The technique can, of course, be made to serve the interest only of those who set the objectives. But cooptation, in its non-pejorative sense, is predicated on the assumption that both the general goals and the general means to attain them must, for the most part, be established by "experts," if the "best" interests of the participants and the community are to be served. The learning process, for instance, is most effective when the instructor guides the students' discussion and research toward a deeper understanding of the discipline in which he specializes. Cooptative participation is also an effective means of rehabilitating groups of persons who lack the knowledge or the built-in desire to help themselves. To nurture in such persons the desire to improve their own situation, without first providing them insights into what goals can be pursued and how, is to leave them exposed to the whims of demagogues.

It follows from this reasoning that, if effective inroads on the poverty problem are to be made, experts in the field must—at least during the formative period—possess sufficient powers of manipulation to control the situation, in order to select the range of "suitable" policy options and to allow for experimentation and innovation (within certain prescribed boundaries). The experts' ultimate objective, however, must be to make themselves superfluous, vacating in favor of leaders indigenous to the participant groups. The route to this final goal is as follows: In the initial stages, citizen participation is construed narrowly, as representation or actual involvement of the poor in formal policy-making and in the development and administration of anti-poverty services.[6] In

6. To be more nearly exact, cooptative participation on this level includes:
   1. Taking part, either as advisers or "voters," in the shaping of anti-poverty policies.

this way, the interest, active involvement, and cooperation of the poverty group is obtained. Over time, indigenous leaders begin to emerge and the participants themselves begin to acquire expertise. Finally, the point is reached when they need neither programs to stimulate participation nor guidance in what they do.

RESEARCH QUESTIONS AND RESEARCH METHODS

The main thrust of our inquiry will be to determine the extent to which the citizen participation aspect of Baltimore's anti-poverty effort has been interest-oriented or cooptative; and whether the citizen-participation effort has yet or is likely in the future to result in a significant reallocation of community values. At a more nearly specific level, we will ask: If participation is primarily cooptative in nature, has it engendered among the poverty population a willingness to support anti-poverty programs and cooptative in their implementation? If not, why not? If so, in what ways is their willingness manifested? Are leaders beginning to emerge from the poverty population? If so, to what extent are they being absorbed into the established political system? And in what degree, if at all, have they become divorced—consciously or unintentionally—from the groups they purportedly lead?

Conversely, if participation is largely interest-oriented, what proportion of those in poverty have developed interests susceptible of defense or promotion through political action? To what extent have they required the resources—power and

2. Taking part, either as advisers or "voters," in planning proposed anti-poverty programs.
3. Taking part in the development and administration of anti-poverty programs.
4. Taking part in the delivery of anti-poverty services.
For purposes which we discuss in the next section, simply being a receiver of anti-poverty services does not constitute participation.

its correlates—to make themselves felt in the political process? And how often have they actually intervened in the process in order to promote their interests, and with what effect? Has acquisition of political interests and resources led them to a militancy that has reached the point where it has produced a reallocation of values more nearly in their favor? Or has their newly found militancy provoked political reaction of various kinds on the part of other groups in the community? In either case, if not, why not?

There are several ways to get at these and related questions. Much useful evidence may be adduced through careful observation of what actually takes place in the political process—trends in voting behavior, the pattern of legislative decisions, the incidence of and reasons for demonstrations and protests, and the like. Face-to-face interviews with key persons in the community may reveal much about which issues are overt and which covert, the nature and extent of the "mobilization of bias" in the community, and the inner workings of the political process.

These and similar methods, useful though they are, give only an imperfect picture of what may be called the "view from below"—the poverty population's own perception of its political interests, resources, and role. To get directly at this aspect of the problem, we shall interview as many as 3000 adults in low-income households, asking them a series of questions designed to test the validity of the following set of propositions:

1. Although most persons in poverty share the predominant values of American society, they have far less faith than most other Americans that their aspirations for a better life can be realized.

2. The great majority of those in poverty are alienated from the established political process, in that they are either openly hostile to it or (more characteristically) believe that there is no way to bring their preferences to bear upon it.

The latter view is crudely expressed as, "You can't fight City Hall."

3. As a consequence, the poor do not believe that citizen participation is a means of obtaining the money and services which will help them gain dignity and a chance to improve their "quality of life."

4. Cooptative participation within the anti-poverty effort can help the poor develop a set of political interests, increase their political resources, and acquire the know-how to intervene effectively in the political process. In other words, cooptative participation by the poor can lead to interest-oriented participation and the development of indigenous leadership.

5. Interest-oriented persons and groups, including many initially activated through cooptative participation within the anti-poverty system, are becoming a significant political force in Baltimore in sustaining and expanding the anti-poverty effort. They are capable of, and to an extent are, exerting political pressure upon both local and national officials for the enlargement of existing programs and for the inauguration of others.

These propositions, taken as a whole, are focused on two questions: How do the size and composition of the programs that make up the anti-poverty system affect the manner and extent of citizen participation of the poor? Conversely, how does citizen participation affect the anti-poverty system? The importance of these questions is based upon the probability that there is a significant relationship between self-respect, economic well-being, and citizen participation. There is considerable evidence that persons who possess a feeling of confidence in dealing with their everyday problems and challenges are more likely to participate in politics.[7] These per-

7. Gordon Allport, "The Psychology of Participation," *Psychological Review*, (May 1945), pp. 117–32; Angus Campbell, "The Passive Citizen," *Acta Sociologica* (fasc. 1–2, 1962), pp. 9–21; Angus Campbell, *et al.*, *The American Voter*

sons are predominantly from middle and upper socio-economic status groups in American society. Conversely, there is substantial evidence that persons who score highly on anomie and alienation tests, those who have a sense of powerlessness, are less likely to be active in political affairs.[8] They have low income and little education. On the basis, however, of two studies conducted in 1961,[9] there is support for the belief that persons who are attempting to improve their socio-economic conditions are inclined to become politically active as part of their effort to move upward. In sum, there is some factual support for the underlying assumption of the proposition stated above: that citizen participation initiated by the anti-poverty programs could make a significant contribution toward the elimination of poverty.

Before we can understand the relationship between citizen participation and the anti-poverty effort, we must know more precisely what citizen participation means *operationally*, what forms it has taken, what interaction there has been between one form and another—such as the interaction, if it indeed exists, between cooptative and interest-oriented participation—and what effects these manifold forms have had upon participants and upon the entire program. Once these areas have been investigated, we will be in a position to relate our analysis of citizen participation of the poor to

(New York, 1960); Robert Lane, *Political Life: Why People Get Involved in Politics* (Glencoe, Ill., 1959); Paul Mussen and R. Wyszynski, "Personality and Political Participation," *Human Relations* (Feb. 1952), pp. 65–82; and Lester Milbrath, *Political Participation* (Chicago, 1965).

8. Herbert Goldhamer, "Public Opinion and Personality," *American Journal of Sociology* (Jan. 1950), pp. 346–54; Robert Lane, *Political Life*, op. cit.; Morris Rosenberg, "Self-Esteem and Concern with Public Affairs," *Public Opinion Quarterly* (Summer 1962), pp. 201–11.

9. Mattei Dogan, "Political Ascent in a Class Society: French Deputies 1870–1958," in D. Marvick (ed.), *Political Decision-Makers* (Glencoe, Ill., 1961), pp. 57–90; D. Marvick and Charles Nixon, "Recruitment Contracts in Rival Campaign Groups," in Marvick, ibid. pp. 193–217. Also see Milbrath, op. cit. pp. 110–41.

the more general political study. We will then want to address ourselves to a second question: How and in what way
has citizen participation of the poor, particularly participation that has been directly or indirectly generated by the
anti-poverty system, affected, and how is it likely to affect in
future, the authority/power distribution in the political system of Baltimore?

To return to the propositions stated above, numbers 1
through 3 will not have to be investigated in detail, because
a large body of prior research amply attests to their validity.
However, the citizen-participation section of the field survey will provide data indicating the extent to which the poverty population has developed a set of interests, feelings of
self-confidence in dealing with problems, and higher aspirations. Data concerning those who have participated will be
compared with similar information about those of the poor
who neither have been exposed to nor have sought benefits
from anti-poverty programs and those of the poor who in
some way have been involved in the programs.

Proposition 4 can be tested by finding out whether there
are significant differences with respect to engagement in political activity among three groups of the poor: (1) those
who have not participated in any anti-poverty programs, either as workers or receivers of benefits, (2) those who receive
benefits and services from anti-poverty programs but do not
participate in policy-making or administration of the programs, and (3) those who actively participate in policy-making or administration. The purpose of testing this hypothesis
is, as we have indicated, to find out if, on the one hand, the
"unexposed" are politically passive and feel powerless, and
if, on the other, the co-optative participants have political
interests and knowledge, and some feeling of confidence that
they can defend or promote their interests. We intend to use
the personal-effectiveness or confidence scale developed by
the Survey Research Center at the University of Michigan,

comparing the scores made on it by all three groups of the poor: the unexposed, the nonparticipant beneficiaries, and the participants.

In testing proposition 4, we are also interested in finding out which anti-poverty agencies and institutions are successful in maximizing participation (taking into account scope, numbers, and effectiveness) and which agencies and institutions are not. These data will be helpful as a basis for discovering ways of obtaining effective citizen participation and for establishing the standards necessary for setting citizen-participation goals.

Proposition 5 can be partially tested and proposition 4 further tested by finding out if the poor become, in the interest-oriented sense, more politically active and join more organizations *after* they have become co-optative participants in the anti-poverty system. To validate these hypotheses, it will also be necessary to interview staff members of anti-poverty groups who have observed the development, if any, of participants (proposition 4) and to interview indigenous leaders and participants in regard to their relationships, if any, and in regard to the aims and aspirations of both groups of leaders (proposition 5). Proposition 5 is addressed to a fundamental question: To what extent is the anti-poverty effort stimulating and creating interest-oriented participation and leadership in the ghettos? It could well be that the significance of the entire anti-poverty effort will turn on the answer to this question.

Proposition 5 can also be partially tested by discovering, through the questionnaire, the extent to which the poor who are involved in one way or another with the anti-poverty system believe that the system is important and should be expanded, and the extent to which they are prepared to exert political pressure on behalf of its expansion.

Index

215